The Decay of Capitalist Civilization

By
Sidney and Beatrice Webb

BOOKS FOR LIBRARIES PRESS
FREEPORT, NEW YORK

First Published 1923
Reprinted 1970

330.122
P2b
c.

STANDARD BOOK NUMBER:
8369-5453-X

LIBRARY OF CONGRESS CATALOG CARD NUMBER:
79-124265

PRINTED IN THE UNITED STATES OF AMERICA

PREFACE

WE may as well forestall the obvious criticism that this little book is not "constructive." It is not intended to supply a plan of reconstruction. For such a plan, in considerable detail, the reader is referred to the works advertised in the final pages; and particularly to *A Constitution for the Socialist Commonwealth of Great Britain,* and, on another plane, *The Prevention of Destitution;* or, in the form of a political program, the pamphlet of the British Labor Party, *Labor and the New Social Order* (33 Eccleston Square, London. Price Threepence).

We gratefully acknowledge the help of various friends, who will excuse the omission of their names. But we cannot refrain from expressing our deepest gratitude to our oldest friend and comrade, Mr. Bernard Shaw, who kindly undertook the revision of the proofs in the midst of a General Election when we were otherwise engaged.

41 GROSVENOR ROAD,
WESTMINSTER, *January* 1923.

CONTENTS

INTRODUCTION

It is one of the illusions of each generation that the social institutions in which it lives are, in some peculiar sense, "natural," unchangeable and permanent. Yet for countless thousands of years social institutions have been successively arising, developing, decaying and becoming gradually superseded by others better adapted to contemporary needs. This book shows how we, the nations claiming to be the most advanced in civilization, are no less subject than our predecessors to this process of perpetual change. Just as the Sumerian, the Egyptian, the Greek, the Roman and the Christian medieval civilizations have passed away, our present capitalist civilization, as mortal as its predecessors, is dissolving before our eyes, not only in that "septic dissolution" diagnosed by the Dean of St. Paul's, brought upon us by war, and curable by genuine peace, but in that slower changing of the epochs which war may hasten, but which neither we nor anything else can hinder. The question, then, is not whether our present civilization will be transformed, but how it will be transformed. It may, by considerate adaptation, be made to pass gradually and peacefully into a new form. Or, if there is angry resistance instead of adaptation, it may crash, leaving mankind painfully to build up a new civilization from the lower level of a stage of social chaos and disorder in which not only the abuses but also the material, intellectual and moral gains of the previous order will have been lost.

Unfortunately many who assent to this general proposition of inevitable change, fail to realize what the social institutions are to which this law of change applies. To them the basis of all possible civilization is private property in a sense in which it is so bound up with human nature, that whilst men remain men, it is no more capable of decay or supersession than the rotation of the earth on its axis. But they misunderstand the position. It is not the sanction and security of personal possessions that forms the foundation of our capitalist system, but the institution of private ownership of the means by which the community lives.

At the risk of pedantry we define our meaning. By the term capitalism, or the capitalist system, or as we prefer, the capitalist civilization, we mean the particular stage in the development of industry and legal institutions in which the bulk of the workers find themselves divorced from the ownership of the instruments of production, in such a way as to pass into the position of wage-earners, whose subsistence, security and personal freedom seem dependent on the will of a relatively small proportion of the nation; namely, those who own, and through their legal ownership control, the organization of the land, the machinery and the labor-force of the community, and do so with the object of making for themselves individual and private gains.

That the land and the other instruments of wealth production should be the private property of a relatively small class of individuals, with hardly more public responsibility attached to it than to the possession of a watch or walking-stick; that this private ownership should constitute the basis of the arrangement on which the rest of the community obtain their livelihood; and that it should carry with it the control and organization of the production and distribution of the commodities and services that are the very life of the nation—and this is what is meant by capitalism—this amazing arrangement, far from being eternal and ubiquitous throughout human history, has become the characteristic feature of the civilization of the United States only within three or four generations; and of Europe only within the last few centuries, through the unregulated squattings of commercial adventure on the derelict sites left by the gradual failure of the feudal system of land tenure and agriculture in the country, and of a relatively less important gild organization of manufacture and trading in the towns. We know that, in Europe, before the feudal system and the craft gilds existed, civilizations were based on different forms of slavery or serfdom, the family or the caste. These in their times seemed as rooted in human nature and as unchangeable as capitalism does. What is more, they lasted many centuries, and were thought out and organized in States and Churches as divine orders of society in which every man, from Emperor and Pope to serf and slave, was responsible to God for the use he made of his opportunities. The commercial squatting which, though it began in England under Henry VII., did not come into power until George III. was king, has never been authorized and organized politically and religiousy in the old enduring fashion. The sages who thought it out as political economists declared that it had no concern with the Churches, and that the lawgivers must not meddle with it: its operations were to be godless and they were to be lawless. On these frankly buccaneering terms it undertook to secure the livelihood of the people, not as its aim, but as an incident of its devotion on principle to the art of getting rich quickly. Its sole claim to toleration was its success in fulfilling that cardinal condition.

It is the thesis of this book that though it never fulfilled the condition completely, and in many places violated it with every circumstance of outrage, yet there was a moment, roughly placeable at the middle of the nineteenth century, when it could claim that, in a hundred years, it had produced, on balance, a surprising advance in material civilization for greatly increased populations. But we must add that from that moment to the present it has been receding from defeat to defeat, beaten ever more and more hopelessly by the social problems created by the very civilization it has built up and the very fecundity it has encouraged. In short, that it began to decay before it reached maturity, and that history will regard capitalism, not as an epoch but as an episode, and in the main a tragic episode, or Dark Age, between two epochs. And, seeing that no individual owner recognizes himself as a dictator, let it be at once added that, as will presently be explained, the dictatorship is a class dictatorship, and each separate capitalist is as helpless in the face of the institution of ownership for private profit as are the wage-earners themselves. His control of the forces of competitive capitalism is, at bottom, no greater than a sailor's control of the wind. But as the institution makes each owner a member of a privileged class, and could be superseded by more advantageous arrangements if the class would give up its privileges, it is not altogether unfair to hold each and every member of the class responsible for the results of these privileges.

The labor and socialist movement of the world is essentially a revolt against the capitalist system of society.

We believe that the most advanced races are to-day, in knowledge, character and intelligence ripe for dispensing with this relation; for the supersession of industrial oligarchy by industrial democracy, and of the motive of pecuniary self-interest by that of public service. We realize that there have been, and over the greater part of the globe still are, other dictatorships more vicious in their motives and more disastrous in their results than the dictatorship of the owners of the instruments of production over the wage-earners. Such are the coercion of slaves by their proprietors, of vanquished races by their conquerors, of whole peoples by autocrats or oligarchies, basing themselves on a monopoly of political power by an individual or by a restricted aristocracy or other minority of race, class or creed. Running in and out of all these systems of oppression, sometimes waning, sometimes waxing, are the domestic tyrannies of the man over the woman, and of the parent over the child. Each of these separate and distinct forms of coercion of one human being by another has been embodied in peculiar economic, political or social laws and conventions: each has provoked, among virile races, its complementary movement of revolt and reform. Socialists, so long as they are true to the democracy in which socialism is rooted, are in sympathy with all these movements and are desirous of promoting them. They realize that, in the normal development of society, the abolition of chattel slavery, the establishment of political democracy, and the emancipation of women, must precede any general adoption of democracy in industry. The existence of one or other of these more obvious despotisms masks the despotism of the owners of the instruments of production over those who are dependent for their livelihood on being permitted to use them, and necessarily diverts attention from the specific evils of capitalism. But the primary purpose of the socialist is to focus attention on the peculiar kind of tyranny now exercised even in the most advanced political democracies, by a relatively small class of rich men over a mass of poor men.

The socialist indictment of the capitalist system of industry, and the society based upon it, has four main counts. History proves that, whilst national poverty may have other causes, whenever and wherever the greater part of the population are divorced from the ownership of the instruments of production, even where the aggregate production is relatively enormous, the bulk of the people live in penury, and large numbers of them are perpetually threatened by starvation. In the second place, this penury and its accompanying insecurity are rendered more hideous and humiliating by the relative comfort and luxury of the proprietary class, and by the shameless idleness of some of its members. The worst circumstance of capitalism is, however, neither the poverty of the wage-earner nor the luxury of the property owner, but, thirdly, the glaring inequality in personal freedom between the property-

less man and the member of the class that "lives by
owning." Hour by hour, day by day, year in and year
out, the two-thirds of the nation who depend for their
daily or weekly housekeeping on gaining access to
the instruments of production find themselves working
under the orders of the relatively restricted class of
those who own these instruments. The sanction for
the orders is not legal punishment, but, ultimately, a
starvation which is supposed to be optional. That is
what is meant by the wage-earners when they complain
of "wage slavery." Fourthly, the socialist believes
that the very basis of the capitalist system is scientifically unsound, as a means of organizing the production
and distribution of commodities and services, and
fundamentally inconsistent with the spiritual advancement of the race.

We shall examine successively the four distinct evils
that socialists believe to be demonstrably inherent in
the capitalist organization of society. We shall deal
first with three of them: the poverty of the poor, the
inequality of incomes, and the disparity in personal
freedom, all of which are invariably found associated
with the divorce of the mass of the people from the
ownership of the instruments of production. We shall
then show that, whilst the capitalist system achieved an
initial success in increasing the wealth of the nation, it
has been eventually found to fail even in maximizing
the production of commodities and services; and thus

not only to defeat its own professed object but also, by its exclusive reliance on the motive of pecuniary gain to individual owners, to be inimical to national morality and international peace; in fact, to civilization itself.

THE DECAY OF CAPITALIST
CIVILIZATION

CHAPTER I

THE POVERTY OF THE POOR

THE outstanding and entirely unexpected result of
the capitalist organization of society is the widespread
penury that it produces in the nation. A whole century of experience, in the most advanced civilizations
of Europe and America alike, reveals this widespread
penury as the outcome, or at least the invariable con-
comitant, of the divorce of the mass of the people from
the ownership of the instruments of production; and
of the aggregation, which has everywhere occurred,
of this ownership in a relatively small propertied class.
It is of course not suggested that a low standard of
livelihood and the imminent peril of starvation is peculiar to capitalism. In more primitive communities,
in which the instruments of production are held in
common, or are widely distributed among those who
gain their livelihood by using them, chronic poverty
and recurrent famines have been in the past, and are
to-day, by no means uncommon. But in these back-
ward societies the meagerness and insecurity of livelihood is attributable either to man's incapacity to control the forces of nature, as manifested in droughts,
floods and diseases; or to the paucity of natural re-

3

sources, such as the lack of fertile land and minerals, or the severity of the climate; or else to the absence of applied science enabling men to use with efficiency the sources of wealth that exist. But the capitalist organization of industry confronts us with a paradox. The countries in which it has been developed in its most complete form enjoy great natural resources and have made great use of science in turning them to the service of man. Taking these nations as wholes, the aggregate wealth thus produced is relatively enormous. Notwithstanding these favorable conditions, the material circumstances of the people, so far as the bulk of them are concerned and taking all things into account, have scarcely been bettered; they have been, sometimes, under unrestrained capitalism, actually worsened. There is reason to suppose that the England of the yeoman cultivator and the master craftsman, with all its privations and all its drawbacks, yielded to an actual majority of its inhabitants, more food, more serviceable clothing, more light, purer air, pleasanter surroundings, and, be it added, in practice even a greater degree of personal freedom, than did the far more productive England of the first half of the nineteenth century, when the " free enterprise " of the owners and organizers of the instruments of production was at its zenith.

THE RESULTS OF THE INDUSTRIAL REVOLUTION

The tragic process of this worsening of the conditions is described in every account of the industrial revolution, when the enthronement of the capitalist as the unrestrained exploiter of land, machinery and human labor was accompanied by results to the common people more terrible in prolonged agony than those of any war. So far as Great Britain is concerned, the account of what happened between 1760 and 1850 has, during the present generation, become a wearisome platitude of the history text-books, not only of the workman's tutorial class but even of the girls' high school. But if we realize what happened it is difficult to write about it without passion. Relays of young children destroyed in the cotton factories; men and women, boys and girls, weakened and brutalized by promiscuous toil in mines and iron-works; whole families degraded by the indecent occupation of the tenement houses of the crowded slums; constantly recurrent periods of under-employment and unemployment, and consequent hunger and starvation; food adulterated, air poisoned, water contaminated, the sights and sounds of day and night rendered hideous: these are the commonplace incidents of the industrial Britain of the beginning of the nineteenth century, discovered and rediscovered, not by sentimental philanthropists and sensational newspaper reporters, but by departmental inspectors and parliamentary inquiries. It is usually forgotten that essentially similar evils are continuing to-day among the industrial populations in the slums of the great cities in America as well as in Europe to an extent that is positively greater in volume than existed under analogous conditions between 1800 and 1840.

Further, the physical suffering, the accidents and the diseases that have been the concomitants of the capitalist system have not been its biggest evil. It is not in material things only that " the destruction of the poor is their poverty." To the hero on the ice-field or the saint in the desert, the lack of adequate means of subsistence, combined with the utmost hardship, may be compatible with the spiritual exaltation, individual development, and the continuous exercise of personal initiative and enterprise. To the peasant cultivator and master-craftsman of primitive communities, a flood, or drought, an epidemic, the murrain or the blight, though it produces devastation and famine, may create fellowship and stimulate energy. But what modern industrialism destroyed, generation after generation, in those who succumbed to it, was the soul of the people. There is a moral miasma as deadly as the physical. Right down to our own day the dwellers in the slums of the great cities of Europe and America, actually in increasing numbers as one generation follows another, find themselves embedded, whether they will it or not, in all the ugliness, the dirt and the disorder of the mean streets. Breathing, from infancy up, an atmosphere of morbid alcoholism and sexuality, furtive larceny and unashamed mendacity—though here and there a moral genius may survive, saddened but unscathed—the average man is, mentally as well as physically, poisoned. The destitution against which the socialist protests is thus a degradation of character, a spiritual demoralization, a destruction of human personality itself.

THE EVILS NOT INTENDED

In the opening sentence of this chapter we described those appalling results of capitalism as unexpected. They are, in fact, too bad to have been intentionally brought about by human beings at any stage of civilization, much less at a period so full of humanitarian and libertarian sentiment and of intelligent progressive aspiration as the period extending from the careers of Voltaire and Rousseau to those of Shelley and Cobden. As the judge in Ibsen's play remarks, " People don't do such things." That nevertheless those things were done, and are still in the doing, is explained by the fact that the first effects of capitalism correspond to certain natural consequences which have an air of justice and propriety agreeable to the uninstructed moral sense of mankind, and are accompanied by the breaking down of restrictions on enterprise the reasonableness of which is apparent to trained statesmen only. If A becomes poor and B becomes rich, other things remaining equal, our sense of justice is shocked and our compassion and indignation aroused. But if simultaneously with the change in relative income A' and his family become repulsively dirty, drunken, and ignorant, and B becomes attractively well-groomed and invites us to share a delightful hospitality at the hands of his charmingly dressed wife and daughters; and if this state of things is clearly and directly traceable to the fact that A is living recklessly beyond his income and B saving money every year, nine hundred and ninety-nine men out of a thousand will conclude that poetic justice demands this very retribution and reward; that A has himself to thank for his poverty, which is a socially wholesome deterrent from his vices; and that all can be as prosperous as B if they will follow his example. And if, in addition, B breaks down a very obvious feudal tyranny, and wins for all persons like himself the political predominance their apparent virtues seem to deserve, an overwhelming impression of progress and enlightenment will be produced.

It is not until the inequalities have gone so far that they are beyond all reason that people began to suspect that A's degradation is effect and not cause, and B's prosperity is cause and not effect. When a baby in one street owns a million pounds actually before it is born, and a woman who has worked hard from her eighth year to her eightieth is removed from another to die in the workhouse, eighteenth-century optimism begins to lose confidence.

But Presently Condoned

But even when the optimism is staggered, it does not surrender. It changes its ground, and begins to argue that the poverty of the poor is the inevitable price of a general improvement in the condition of mankind. There seems to be no limit to the willingness of fortunate men—even men of high ideals and great devotion—to accept excuses for the suffering of other people, so long as this suffering seems to be necessary to the maintenance of the position or the interests of their class or race. There were men of exceptionally fine character and intellect among the slave-owning legislators of the Southern States of America who were, right down to Lee's surrender at Appomattox Court House, passionately convinced that slavery and the slave market formed the only possible basis for the social order that seemed to them indispensable to civilization. In the universities as well as in the armies of Germany in 1914-18 there were men of high morality and trained intelligence who honestly regarded the invasion of neutral Belgium, the devastation of occupied

areas, the enforcement of labor on civilians, and the
sinking of passenger ships, as regrettable necessities
incidental to the fulfillment of Germany's civilizing mission as the dominating world-power. In like manner
we watch such patriots as Bright and Cobden, with
their following of well-intentioned capitalists, condon-
ing and justifying conditions of employment and
housing which were almost as degrading as the chattel
slavery they were denouncing, and which resulted, in
England alone, in far more preventable disease and
deaths in a single year than all the casualties of the
Crimean war. And it was not only the business men
and slum landlords who tolerated and defended this
mass of misery and degradation. In the England of
the first half of the nineteenth century, as in the Germany of the Great War, men of science and men of
God—" instructors and chaplains of a pirate ship "—
justified the actions of the practical men of their own
world. The horrors of the unregulated factory, the
mine and slum—made abstract in what was called
" the natural rate of wages "—were defended by
Ricardo and Nassau Senior among the intellectuals,
by the Rev. Thomas Malthus and Archbishop Whately
among the priests, as the last discoveries of the science
of political economy, and part and parcel of the Law
of God as manifested in the doctrines of the Christian Church. " Without a large proportion of poverty," England was told by the inventor of the modern

police system and leading authority on " the resources of the British Empire," " there could be no riches, since riches are the offspring of labor, while *labor can result only from a state of poverty.* Poverty is that state and condition of society where the individual has no surplus labor in store, or, in other words, no property or means of subsistence but what is derived from the constant exercise of industry. *Poverty is therefore a most necessary and indispensable ingredient in society, without which nations and communities could not exist in a state of civilization.* It is the lot of man. It is the source of wealth, since without poverty there could be no labor, no riches, no refinement, no comfort, and no benefit to those who may be possessed of wealth, inasmuch as, without a large proportion of poverty, surplus labor could never be rendered productive in procuring either the conveniences or luxuries of life." [1]

[1] *Resources of the British Empire,* by Patrick Colquhoun, 1914, quoted in *A History of British Socialism,* by M. Beer, vol. i, p. 145.
" The palm in this line belongs to the English economist, the Rev. J. Townsend, who wrote under the name 'The Well-wisher of Mankind' against the Poor Law. In his masterpiece, which lived to see a second edition—*A Dissertation on the Poor Laws* (London, 1817), pp. 39-41, quoted by Marx, *Capital,* vol. i, pp. 602, 603—he explains to us that the poor are improvident and multiply rapidly in order 'that there may always be some to fulfill the most servile, the most sordid and the most ignoble offices in the community. The stock of human happiness is thereby much increased, whilst the more delicate are not only relieved from drudgery . . . but are left without interruption to pursue those callings which are suited to their various dispositions.' The Poor Law 'tends to destroy the harmony and beauty, the symmetry and order of that system which God and Nature have established in the world'" (*Marxism v. Socialism,*

The Modern Apologia

It must not be imagined that this callousness to the suffering of the "common people," on the part of kindly natures and otherwise good citizens, is merely an incident of the past. Any one who takes the trouble to observe the minds of the people around him, of the "well-to-do" or comfortable class, in Britain or France, Australia or the United States, whether manufacturers or mere dividend-receivers, statesmen or professors, will easily discover how complacently they assume, as a matter of course, first, that the relative position of the property owners and the propertyless has some real though undefined relation to their several deserts or racial qualities; and secondly, that, whether or not this is the case, the existence of an extensive propertyless class is a necessary condition of their own exemption from manual toil and their wide opportunities for personal initiative, which are deemed indispensable for civilization and culture. Thus a tacit acceptance of the penury, the continuing privations, and, as regards a large proportion of the wage-earners, the always imminent peril of want, as the lot of the bulk of the population, even in the richest countries, has survived the full realization both of the existence of these

by Vladimir G. Simkovitch, 1913, p. 107). The reverend author was "rector of Pewsey, Wilts, and chaplain to Jean, Duchess Dowager of Atholl." His *Dissertation on the Poor Laws* was first published in 1786, and was more than once reprinted during the ensuing thirty years.

evils and of their causal connection with capitalism.
We remember being startled by an astute Japanese
statesman casually observing that " the introduction of
the capitalist system into Japan had brought in its train
an ever-growing class of destitute persons—a class
quite unknown in the old Japan of the daimio and the
rice cultivator. This destitution," he added, with a
philosophic smile, " is the price which Japan has had to
pay for increasing the personal wealth of her leading
citizens, and for becoming a world power."

It is unnecessary to dwell in greater detail upon the
poverty of the poor as the most obvious evil result of
the " free enterprise " of the profit-making capitalist.
Thinkers and statesmen of all shades of opinion nowadays recognize this poverty, and with more or less
alacrity apply the remedial measures in limitation of
the freedom of capitalist enterprise which they have
learnt from the socialists of the past two or three generations, in an attempt to mitigate what they deplore.
But these mitigations do not exhaust the problem. It
is only the first achievement of socialist thought to
have got accepted in Great Britain and Australasia,
and, in all that has followed from Robert Owen's plea
for factory legislation, to some extent applied, the
essentially socialist policy of deliberately maintaining
by law a national minimum of civilized life throughout the whole community. By a full adoption of this
policy, as is now widely recognized, the nation can, if

it chooses, prevent the recurrence of any widespread destitution. It can even put an end, so far as it is a case of a whole class, to the insecurity of livelihood which verges on destitution.[1] To accomplish even so much, if the statesmen would only take the task in hand, would be an enormous gain. But this process of leveling up, within the capitalist system, all sections of the community to a prescribed minimum standard of life—say to that of the skilled engineer in regular employment, or that of the assistant teacher in a public elementary school—will not, in itself, diminish, and, as we shall point out, may in the long run even increase the inequality, alike in material circumstances and in personal freedom, between the relatively small class of persons who own and organize the instruments of production and the mass of people whose livelihood depends on being permitted to use them.

[1] For a full exposition of this policy and its application in practical detail, see *The Prevention of Destitution*, by S. and B. Webb, 1920.

CHAPTER II

INEQUALITY OF INCOME

WE believe that, apart from the poverty of the poor, so gross a disparity between the income of one citizen and another as is inherent in the present advanced stage of the capitalist organization of industry, is in itself injurious to the commonwealth. The extremes of inequality are known to all men. In every newspaper, capitalist or labor, we find now and again sensational paragraphs drawing attention to the gross disparity in the incomes of selected individuals—between the few shillings or dollars a week of the laboring man or woman, and the hundreds of thousands of pounds or millions of dollars a year credited to the super-capitalists of Great Britain and the United States. But a more significant fact is the inequality in the way in which the national income is shared between one class of society and another.[1] To take, as a leading instance,

---

[1] "Inequality" of income may, of course, be understood in several ways (as to which see *Some Aspects of the Inequality of Incomes in Modern Communities*, by Hugh Dalton, 1920). As to the statistics, see the estimates of various authorities quoted in Fabian Tract No. 5, *Facts for Socialists; Riches and Poverty*, by Sir Leo Chiozza-Money, 1905; *British Incomes and Property*, second edition, 1921, and *Wealth and Taxable Capacity*, 1922, both by Sir Josiah Stamp; and *Changes in the Distribution of Income, 1880-1913*, 1918, and *The Division of the Product of Industry*, 1919, both by A. L. Bowley.

the United Kingdom at its wealthiest period—the years immediately preceding the Great War. The inhabitants of this country were then producing, in the aggregate, each year, commodities and services priced at a total, in round numbers, of two thousand million pounds, besides drawing a couple of hundred millions of pounds a year from investments in other countries. One-half of this aggregate of commodities and services, out of which the whole people had to live, was taken by the one-ninth of the community which was at that date liable to income tax, comprising, therefore, all the families that had as much as £160 a year income. Nearly one-third of the remaining half (say, three hundred millions sterling) fell to the share of that *nouvelle couche sociale,* the black-coated proletariat of humble clerks and teachers and minor officials, along with the smallest shopkeepers and traders—comprising, with their families, the two-ninths of the population who were not manual working wage-earners, but who nevertheless did not get for their work as much as £160 a year per family. There remained, out of the aggregate product, for the two-thirds of the population who were manual working wage-earners and their families, somewhere about eight hundred millions, which, after making the necessary deductions for sickness and other spells of unemployment, worked out, for the adult male worker, at an average weekly income throughout the year of something like twenty-five shillings on which to maintain his family. And this glaring inequality in the distribution of the national income was not peculiar to the United Kingdom, or to those particular years. It is characteristic of every capitalist society. The statistics for France, so far as they can be ascertained, were no less extreme in their inequality. Those for the German Empire were apparently much the same. Even in the United States, with all the boundless resources of North America, there stood revealed, so far as the statistics extend, a parallel inequality in the way the national income was shared. To put it another way: in 1890 the total income of that country was so divided that 40 per cent was received as the reward of owning, and 60 per cent as the reward of doing.[1]

THE NATION "CHOOSES INEQUALITY"

It is therefore clear that a nation, in deciding to establish or to continue the private ownership of land and capital as the basis of the industrial organization of its people, deliberately chooses inequality. We must face this now with our eyes open. The outrageous disparity in capitalist countries between one man and another, and between one class and another, independently of their merits, and often in the inverse ratio of their industry and social utility, is not pro-

[1] *Americanised Socialism*, by James Mackaye, 1918.

duced by any defect in the working of capitalism, but is inherent in its very nature. It is not a transient phenomenon, but a permanent feature. By leaving in almost unrestrained private ownership practically all the differential factors in wealth production—such portions of its land and capital as are for the time being more advantageous than the worst in economic use—we cause the resultant " rent " or surplus value, to the extent, as the statistics indicate, of at least a third of the aggregate product, to fall into the lap of the more fortunately situated members of the property-owning class, irrespective of their rendering any service whatsoever to the community. " The widow," says Carlyle, " is gathering nettles for her children's dinner: a perfumed seigneur, delicately lounging in the *Œil de bœuf,* has an alchemy whereby he will extract from her the third nettle, and name it Rent and Law." A similar " surplus value " over and above the maintenance conceded to the workers concerned is being produced, year in, year out, throughout all capitalist industry down to the marginal cultivation in each case. This statement does not imply that " all wealth is created by labor," meaning manual labor. The mining engineer, the captain of the merchant ship, the passenger superintendent of the railway, the bank manager, the literary or scientific writer or teacher, the inventor, the designer, the organizer, and those who under various names actually spend their lives in ini-

tiating and directing enterprises of social utility, together with the innumerable other "brain-working"
participants, may all be assumed to be coöperating in
the making of the product, and to be legitimately earning a maintenance for their families and themselves.
How far their several incomes bear any relation to the
social values of their respective services is a disputable
question, to which no convincing answer has been
found. But, apart from all these incomes, there is
normally a surplus accruing to the class of legal owners of the instruments of production, merely as a consequence of this ownership, irrespective of whether or
not they are the organizers or directors, or are otherwise coöperating in production in any way whatsoever.
This surplus goes, in fact, in all capitalist societies,
very largely, and as it seems, even increasingly, to persons who are not, in respect of this income, producing
anything. It will be obvious that this incident of the
individual ownership of the differential factors in
wealth production—of the soils, sites, mines, factories,
and shops superior in productivity to the worst in
economic use, or, where agreements or amalgamations
among most of the separate proprietors have led to
monopoly, of the tribute on the consumers that this
monopoly permits—is not dependent on the lowness of
wages: it remains unaffected by the remedial expedient of raising every member of the community to a
prescribed national minimum. In so far as any such

mitigation of the poverty of the poor increases their
efficiency in wealth production, and thereby the aggregate output, the total of " rent " may even be increased.
If the widow is enabled to gather seven nettles instead
of three, the seigneur lounging in the *Œil de bœuf*
may find himself extracting from her more nettles than
before.

The Law of Inheritance

And the effect of this diversion of a large part of the
national product to the mere payment for ownership
is cumulative. The small rentier may consume all his
dividends in supporting himself and his family, but the
larger the rent-roll or dividends the greater is normally the balance over personal expenditure, a balance
automatically invested, through the highly organized
banking and financial system, in additional instruments
of production, yielding still further dividends. The
possessor of what may be deemed a moderate fortune
may lose it or dissipate it; but nearly all the super-
capitalists know how to secure themselves and their
heirs against any such calamity. Hence it is now
axiomatic that, under the reign of capitalism, those
who own the most, not those who work the most, get,
in fact, the largest incomes; and those who own the
least get, in fact, the smallest incomes, however hard
they work. And the gulf is always widening. It is
this automatic heaping up of individual fortunes—by

the older economists termed, apparently with unconscious irony, "the reward of abstinence"—that accounts for that ever-multiplying monstrosity of capitalist civilization—the millionaire. Moreover, under the laws of inheritance that all capitalist nations have devised or developed, the payment for ownership not only intensifies the inequality of income between contemporaries, but also creates an hereditary class of property owners, the members of which find themselves legally entitled to levy, generation after generation, to the end of time, a tribute upon the toil of their contemporary fellow citizens. It is necessary to emphasize this point. *The ownership of land and capital by private individuals, coupled with the legal institution of inheritance, is bound to result, however much it may be humanized by philanthropy and restrained from the worst excesses by a systematic application of the Policy of the National Minimum, in a division of the community into two permanent and largely hereditary castes—a nation of the rich and a nation of the poor.*

The evil effects of this gross inequality between the incomes of individuals and of classes are manifold, They may be summarized under four main heads: an altogether inefficient consumption of the commodities and services annually available for the nation's maintenance; the encouragement of parasitic idleness; and, consequent on these, a widespread lack of good man-

ners and a constantly operating dysgenic influence on
the race.

The Inefficient Consumption of Wealth

" For anything I know," wrote the second President
of the United States to Jefferson, " this globe may be
the Bedlam, *le Bicêtre,* of the universe." [1] The events
of the last hundred years almost seem to strengthen
the suggestion that, in a universe of transmigrating
souls, our particular planet may have been assigned to
be the lunatic asylum for the solar system. At least,
the way in which the most civilized communities upon
our globe consume or use the commodities and services
produced by the arduous daily toil of their millions of
men and women, appears to be consistent with this
hypothesis. We are not referring to the delirium of
social lunacy of the four years of the Great War of
1914-18, during which nearly all capitalist governments
of the world used up the entire product of the labor of
their respective nations, devastated fertile land, burnt
innumerable buildings, and deliberately destroyed
plant and machinery, in order to kill and maim some
thirty millions of the youngest and strongest of their
male adults. Let us think, rather, of the normal consumption of the annual product in peace time—a con-

---

[1] John Adams to Thomas Jefferson, July 16, 1814; in *The
Works of John Adams,* by C. E. Adams, 1851-6, vol. x, p. 101.

sumption which is taken for granted, and accepted by
the well-to-do citizen with the same sort of self-complacency as is the illusion of being God Almighty by
the peaceful lunatic.

THE REPORT OF THE COSMIC INSPECTOR

Imagine the report of the Spirit Expert in Scientific
Consumption deputed by the government of the ALL
GOOD to investigate the progress towards sanity of
the inmates of the planetary lunatic asylum. " I cannot agree," he writes, " with my colleague, the Inspector of Scientific Production, that the inhabitants
of the Earth are showing any approach to sanity. I
need not discuss what is sanity. It will be remembered
that we are forbidden, by our instructions, to inquire
into the ultimate aims or ideals of the Earthians, seeing that the rightness of ends as distinguished from
means has always been a matter of controversy even
in the Court Circle of the ALL GOOD. I take as the
test of the sanity of individuals or races, sanctioned by
the law of the universe, the capacity of selecting the
appropriate means to a given end, as verified by the
subsequent event. The end or ideal of the Earthians
is not in dispute. They are never tired of asserting to
each other, with fatuous smiles, that the end they have
in view is the health and happiness of the whole community. They admit that, in the earthly state, this de-

pends, in the first place, on the effective application of the necessary commodities and services. My colleague tells me that, in the production of most commodities and of some services, they are showing signs of increasing intelligence in the use of materials and the organization of manual labor and brainwork. In the consumption of wealth they seem to me to be going from bad to worse. Former generations produced less, but what they did produce they seem to me to have consumed more intelligently. Take the three primary necessities of earthly life—food, shelter and clothing. I first made it my business to review the consumption of clothing. In the Idle Quarter, there were a number of women, each of whom prided herself on consuming in the manufacture of her garments the whole year's toil of from one hundred to two hundred garment workers. I overheard one of them say, in a debate on possible economies, that the whole annual product of one worker would barely suffice to supply her ' with a hat and a nightgown.' A younger woman, about to be married, had provided herself, for her exclusive use, of no fewer than seventy-nine nightgowns, besides other garments on which many hundreds of persons had worked for more than a year. In order to consume the toil of one or two hundred persons on the garments of one woman, labor had to be wasted in barbaric decoration, in using materials which would not last long in wear, and in providing separate suits for each occasion (I observed one woman, closely attended by a worker, changing her clothes five times in the day); and, most idiotic of all, in discarding whole wardrobes of garments once or twice a year in order to introduce a new fashion. As Earthians are apparently valued according to their capacity to consume without producing, this inefficient consumption of the garment workers' toil was imitated by women of more limited means, so that the clothing of the whole population reflected the fantastic and unhygienic habits of the wealthy members. Passing from the Idle Quarter to the homes of the garment workers themselves, I found these persons living day and night in the same clothes—ugly, badly fitting, scanty and foul. Their children were attending school in leaky boots; and, in hot weather and cold alike, were wearing rags of the same thickness and texture. The explanation was simple. These makers of garments were each of them restricted, for the whole year, to what could be produced by a single person working for one, two, or three weeks, as against the hundred or two hundred persons working for fifty-two weeks to equip each woman of the Idle Quarter. This example is typical. Hence, as a means to attain the end of the health and happiness of the whole community, the consumption of clothing on Earth cannot but be considered as a symptom of insanity.

" Then as to the shelter which the climate of these

parts of the Earth makes essential. The homes in the Idle Quarters are often so large, and contain so many empty rooms, that the constant labor of from five to twenty-five persons is required merely to keep them clean, and to serve the daily needs of the so-called occupiers, who might or might not have wives and children to share them. Meantime, even in the wealthiest cities, 20 per cent of the total population are herded together in one- or two-roomed tenements. I actually discovered a number of cases of two or more families working and living in a single room, the resulting indecency and disease being unfit for publication.

"Even in the matter of food—the one absolute necessary for continued existence on Earth, the consumption is madly inefficient. It is noteworthy that the Earthians have now discovered the facts with regard to the consumption of food. They know, within a narrow margin, exactly the quantity and quality of food required for healthy, human existence; they know that less than this means starvation and more than this means disease. And yet, if we compare the normal consumption of food-values of the bulk of the inhabitants with the normal consumption of food-values in the Idle Quarters, measured in the labor required for their production, we find it ranging in the proportion of something like one to twenty, with the result that the mass of the people, and those who are working hardest, are habitually undernourished, whilst a select few, who are very often absolutely unproductive, are not only wasting food, but are actually making themselves inert and deformed in consuming it."

So far the imaginary report of the Spirit Inspector on Earthian Consumption. The mundane economist not merely confirms this criticism but even pushes it further. The present inequality of income conspicuously leads, not only to inefficient consumption, but also to the production of wrong commodities. The power of commanding from the world just what commodities and services the several owners of the unequal incomes elect to enjoy, vitiates, at a blow, all the assumptions of the earlier economists that production would, on the whole, be automatically directed to the satisfaction of human needs, *in the order of their urgency*. It gives us the state of things in which a vast amount of labor is lavished on the most futile luxuries, whilst tens of thousands of infants are perishing from lack of milk, innumerable children are growing up without adequate nurture, millions of men and women find themselves condemned to starved and joyless lives, and the most urgent requirements of the community as a whole—to say nothing of the essentials to the well-being of future generations—remain unprovided for. Under a system of private property in the means of production, the " effective demand " of individuals affords no sort of assurance of the fulfillment of the most indisputable national needs.

The Vitiation of Effective Demand

Unfortunately this is as true of the one-third or the two-fifths of the total income which makes up the expenditure of the toiling masses, as of the vastly larger incomes dispensed by the middle and upper classes. To quote the words of an American writer: "Under present conditions the bad example of the rich is a greater evil than their indulgence, because it spreads inefficiency so widely. The effort to imitate or keep pace with the idle rich is infectious and demoralizes even the poor. It breeds luxurious habits, not only among those who can afford them, but among those who cannot. Obviously this has a very depressing effect on consumptive efficiency throughout the community." [1]

The Wastefulness of Consumption

It is, indeed, amazing that there should have been so much study of the means of increasing the aggregate production of commodities and services, and so little attention to the manner in which they are consumed or used. Yet the very utility of any commodity depends on the way in which it passes into consumption. It is obvious that a given aggregate of commodities and services may result in much more if it is

[1] *Americanised Socialism,* by James Mackaye, 1918.

consumed and used in one way than in another. This
is plain, so far as the organization of an industry is
concerned, to every administrator. The "captain of
industry," applying to his enterprise what he calls
" scientific management," is keenly aware that his task
is so to direct motive and stimulus in the whole staff,
and so to apply to his processes all the resources of
science, as to secure that the raw material, the various
components, the sources of power, and the available
labor-force shall be employed in such a way that the
greatest possible total result is produced from a given
supply. But he will return after his day's work to his
" well-appointed " home—the " appointment " of
which probably consists essentially in avoiding all
labor-saving appliances and making necessary a whole
group of domestic servants—to eat an unwholesome
dinner on which ten times as much labor has been expended as on the meal by which his laborers maintain
their health; and to encourage his wife to crowd his
house with indiscriminate articles of furniture and or-
namentation which have no merit beyond the amount
of labor that has been wasted on them. In " good
times," he will respond to every caprice of his wife and
children, " Get it, it only costs money." The contrast
between the economical " routing " towards maximum production of every item in his factory, and the
thoughtless application of the products themselves,
when they come before him as, within the limits of his

own income, a check-writing director of consumption, can only be characterized as extraordinary. To any observer of the operations of a factory, it will be obvious that five tons of coal wastefully consumed do not constitute so large an item in the national wealth as three tons used in such a way as to produce a larger product. What is true of the consumption of fuel in a factory is equally true of the consumption of individual consumers of the factory's products. Thus, even with regard to national wealth, it is quite incorrect to say that its amount depends wholly on national production. The aggregate wealth of the nation can be as much augmented by an improvement in consumption as by a mere increase in production. The introduction of " summer time "—to give only one instance —is roughly estimated to have represented to the United Kingdom the equivalent of twenty million pounds annually; or as much as the whole product of one of its coalfields.

THE EFFECT OF " RATIONING "

That the great inequality of incomes, which is an inevitable result of private ownership in the means of production, leads, in itself, to a flagrantly wasteful consumption of the aggregate product, has now been recognized by the modern economist. Quite apart from the fact that it destroys all possibility of " marshaling the assets," in such a way that all the most urgent needs of the community may be supplied before the less urgent, the very glorification of expenditure as expenditure leads to the purchase and consumption of commodities merely because they are costly. What is even of greater permanent importance is that there is practically no inducement to discover in what way the available production can be employed to greatest advantage. Hence, until the stress of the Great War drove our statesmen temporarily to think, there was, in Britain as in the United States, neither research nor education in the question of efficient consumption. In Britain, the temporary system of rationing the rich and poor alike, so far as regards some essential food-stuffs, had as one of its great advantages, that persons with leisure, training and opportunity devoted themselves to discovering, not only the obviously useful facts as to food values and food preparation, but also labor-saving appliances in homes, and a more econom-ical and hygienic fashion in clothes. It is suggested that an equally stringent " rationing," not of meat and sugar, but of family incomes, would have had even more useful results. All the ingenuity and devotion of the wealthy women housekeepers might then have been diverted from a rivalry in conspicuous expendi-ture to an emulation in discovery of how to maintain the most charming home on the prescribed equal in-comes! We suggest, indeed, to those to whom art is

foremost, that an entirely new aspect would be given
to design and workmanship, and to the construction
and furnishing of homes, if every consumer, the most
gifted and fastidious as well as the most reckless in
expenditure, could escape the temptations of lavish
cost and transient fashion, and found himself confronted with the problem of how to get the necessary
utility and the greatest beauty out of the expenditure
of the socially prescribed income available for every
family.

The Encouragement of Parasitic Idleness

In times of unemployment and increasing vagrancy
the wage-earners are perpetually reminded that " it is
a law of nature and morality that if a man does not
work neither shall he eat." To enforce this law of
nature and morality we see the country studded with
such brutalizing institutions as the Able-bodied Test
Work-house, the Casual Ward, and, in the last resort,
the jail. With characteristic modesty the spokesmen
of the insurgent unemployed have hitherto replied that
the obligation to work on the part of an individual
citizen must necessarily depend on his being granted
the opportunity; and, greatly daring, the Labor Party
has introduced into the British Parliament a " Right
to Work Bill." The socialist declares that a more
correct answer to the middle-class criticism would be

the enactment of an " Obligation to Work Law," providing that any adult able-bodied person who was discovered not actively engaged in work of national importance should be—not cruelly punished by imprisonment in an Able-bodied Test Workhouse, a Casual
Ward, or a jail—but, with all courtesy, deprived of
the income which enables him to live in idleness. The
socialist believes that the establishment by law of a
class legally enabled to live idly on rent and dividends
amounts to the establishment in the community of a
set of persons who are privileged, and thereby almost
irresistibly tempted, to place themselves habitually
above " the law of nature and morality that if a man
does not work neither shall he eat." The loss to the
community which such social parasitism entails is serious enough, but the effect on the parasites themselves
is even more disastrous. Those who are " above the
law " do not, as we have already seen, escape an extraordinary callousness and insolence, none the less injurious because they are usually themselves unaware of
it, which makes the sufferings of those who do not
belong to their own class seem as unreal and as un-
substantial as if they were the sufferings of another
species. The crippled conscience of the propertied
class is blind to the truism that the man or woman
who consumes without personally contributing to the
world in the production of services or commodities is
a social parasite for whose very presence the world is

the poorer. Consciously or unconsciously such a person, not being infirm or superannuated, is, as Ruskin vainly taught, a thief; and a thief whose depredations are none the less real, and nowadays none the less resented, in that they are made with the sanction of the law. Even the intellect of the parasitic class is affected. This may be seen, not merely in the fact that it is not the families which have inherited millions that usually produce either scientific discoverers or geniuses in art or literature. Only by a subtle deadening of intellect can it be explained why it is almost impossible to make the average wealthy person even understand, still less believe, the obvious economic truth that the world is actually the poorer, not merely by the amount of the food and clothes that he consumes without equivalent personal production, but also by all that he spends on his personal desires and caprices; that, in his case, " spending money " is not only not " good for trade," but actually represents the abstraction from the world's stock of the services and commodities maintaining all those whom, by his purchases, he " commandeers " to his behests, which might otherwise have been devoted to the improvement of the narrow circumstances of the average citizen or to the advancement of science and the cultivation of the arts. It needed all the shock of the Great War to open the intellects of a small proportion of the wealthy to this truth; and they, it is to be feared, have now let it pass out of their minds.

THE LIFE OF UNCONSCIOUS THEFT

This life of unconscious theft, of which the idle
members of the propertied class have an uneasy suspicion, together with the callousness and insolence that
it breeds, as regards the sufferings of any but those
who belong to their own class—subtly degrading as it
is to the rich, has its obverse in its effect on the minds
and characters of those who have not been able, in
the same way, to place themselves above the world's
law. The resulting servility, on the one hand, and on
the other, the envy, or even the simple-minded admira-
tion for a life which is essentially contrary to all principles of morality, is as demoralizing to the poor as it
is to the rich. The bounties of the rich to the poor
actually make matters worse for both of them. All
charity—apart from personal friendship—is demoralizing to giver and receiver alike; and gifts among
those who feel themselves socially unequal carry with
them, however well-intentioned and well-devised, the
poisons of patronage and parasitism. The habitual respect and deference given to men and women who are
wealthy, merely because of their wealth—irrespective
of goodwill, personal charm, or artistic or intellectual
achievements—is as damaging to those who are thus
respected and deferred to, as it is to those who pay
this homage to riches. Not the least of its evils is that
it falsifies social values, and actually obstructs the rec-

ognition, and therefore the imitation, of the qualities of character and intellect that are in themselves admirable. It is not too much to say that, in the Britain or the United States of to-day, the very existence, in any neighborhood, of a non-producing rich family, even if it is what it calls well conducted, is by its evil example a blight on the whole district, lowering the standards, corrupting the morality, and to that extent counteracting the work alike of the churches and the schools.

"ABOVE THE LAW"

If the man himself works for a living, in business or finance, law or administration, but receives for his services an income which places him among the wealthy, he may, by the daily service that he renders, be saved from some of the personal demoralization; though the exaggerated respect which he is paid by reason of his large income brings its own perils. But his wife and children can hardly escape the various results of their own habitual over-consumption and under-employment. The occupation of the wife will almost certainly be socially unproductive, whilst the climate of servility which she meets in household and shop is dangerously enervating. The children grow up in a corrupting atmosphere of material luxury. They cannot escape the feeling, though it may never actually come into their intellectual consciousness, that they are, in the sense already explained, "above the law." The formal schooling that they receive is itself perverted by the class atmosphere. Such of them as are not quite exceptionally gifted with ambition, with a passion for self-sacrifice, or with that intellectual curiosity which is the well-spring of science, almost inevitably content themselves, if they take up any occupation at all, with "walking through the part" which the family position has obtained for them; achieving with a demoralizing mediocrity of effort only mediocre results; and practicing, in fact, throughout life, a policy of "ca' canny" of which a craftsman would be ashamed. Nor are matters improved by the makeshift occupations—philanthropic, artistic or merely social—which untrained and undisciplined men and women of leisure miscall their work. What is required for intellectual and moral hygiene, as well as for equity, is that, in return for all the "orders" on the world that any person gives by the expenditure of his income in a particular way, he should set himself, by his own personal service, to fulfill the "orders" that other members of the community give, or would give if they had at their own disposal their reasonably fair shares of the national income. If he prefers to "live his own life," not obeying other people's orders, let him at least refrain from giving orders; that is, from consuming more than he himself produces. Other economic relations between one man and another mean a self-deception and a self-complacency which is nauseous.[1] It is extraordinary that the in-

[1] The ablest monograph on this subject has been produced in the United States (*The Theory of the Leisure Class*, by Thorstein Veblen, 1899), tracing the origin of a leisure class from ancient civilizations based on a double method of acquiring wealth, viz., the "honorable method of seizure and conversion," *i.e.* hunting, war, predatory raids on and oppression of inferior races; and the "dishonorable method" of personal toil (agriculture and manufacture) enforced on women and on slaves. This tradition was carried on, with modifications, through feudal civilization, the wives and daughters of the nobles (themselves still engaged in the honorable method of seizure and conversion) being exempt from all useful occupations, and becoming "ladies." "From this point on, the characteristic feature of leisure-class life is a conspicuous exemption from all useful employment. . . . Abstention from labor is the conventional mark of social wealth, and is therefore the conventional mark of social standing; and this insistence on the meritoriousness of wealth leads to a more strenuous insistence on leisure. . . . Prescription ends by making labor not only disreputable in the eyes of the community, but morally impossible to the noble, freeborn man, and incompatible with a worthy life" (*ibid.*, pp. 40-41). In modern capitalism the male pursues gain, not by manual labor, which remains dishonorable, but by direction, organization, bargaining, and speculation—all expressions of the conqueror or exploiter—but he insists on the vicarious leisure of his women-kind, and sometimes of his sons, as the hall-mark of his social position. The utility of conspicuous leisure, and consumption for the purpose of establishing social status lies in the element of waste—the ability to bear pecuniary loss. "Time is consumed non-productively (1) from a sense of the unworthiness of productive work, and (2) as an evidence of pecuniary ability to afford a life of idleness" (*ibid.*, p. 43). To this was added luxurious expenditure. "Conspicuous consumption of valuable goods is a means of reputability to the gentleman of leisure. As wealth accumulates on his hands, his own unaided effort will not avail to sufficiently put his opulence in evidence by this method. The aid of friends and competitors is therefore brought in by resorting to the giving of valuable presents and expensive feasts and entertainments" (*ibid.*, p. 75). The chapters on "Conspicuous Leisure," "Conspicuous Consumption," "The Pecuniary Standard of Living," "Pecuniary Canons of Taste," "Dress as an Expression of the Pecuniary Culture," "The Conservation of Archaic Traits," and "Modern Survivals of Prowess" are full of significance as illustrating the culture of a leisure class in a capitalist state.

dividualist philosophers who are always dilating on the bracing effects of competition for a livelihood, as tested by market values, should accept with equanimity the demoralization and degradation which, on their own showing, a life of parasitism imposes upon the offspring of those whom these same philosophers regard as having proved themselves to belong to the finest stocks. It is not easy to see how such reasoners escape the inference that the progress of the community and of the race imperatively demands the abolition, as regards dividend-producing wealth, of the right of inheritance, and with it the opportunity of living without work; if only in order that the young people of each generation—even their own children—may not be deprived of the beneficent results of the competitive struggle.

THE LACK OF GOOD MANNERS

But there is another and quite opposite justification for inequalities in income and personal freedom, which is nowadays more often pertinaciously held than openly expressed. It is very widely felt that good manners, a high standard of refinement, personal charm and even human dignity, are dependent on the existence of a set of families, all the better if hereditary, who are " above the law " of nature and morality that he who does not work shall not eat. The very hallmark of the " gentleman " and the " lady " of to-day is the absence in their daily lives of any need for personal drudgery, for obedience to the commands of others, and for incessant regard to pecuniary considerations; the whole resulting in a freedom to develop new faculties of social advantage, though not productive of exchangeable commodities or services. Combined with this is the attraction, as an individual quality, of an easy habit of command, a form of personal dignity often accompanying the habitual ultilization, virtually coercive, of other people's services.

The Corollary of Bad Manners

We note in passing that those who advertise the social benefit of an aristocracy of good manners, to be based, as an indispensable foundation, on wealth and freedom from any enforceable obligation of service, seem to regard as of no consequence the deterioration of manners brought about by the combination, in the daily lives of the vast majority of the race, of poverty and servility. In the modern industrial state, whether of the Old World or of the New, we see the obverse of the "gentleman" and the "lady" in the typical denizens of the urban slum. The brutality, the coarseness, the inconsiderate noises, the mean backbiting and quarrelsomeness that characterize no small proportion of all the residential quarters open to the wage-earning population compel the more "respectable" of their inhabitants, as they say, to "keep themselves to themselves," because they find social intercourse impossible. It is a pathetic incident of the "bad manners" that—far more than selfishness, cruelty or failure of mutual help—characterize the slums that every one insists on being termed a "gentleman" or "lady"; whilst the honorable appellation of man or woman is used only, with an adjectival swear-word, as a term of abuse!

But the fact we want to emphasize is not the brutalization of the poor but the vulgarization of the rich. We deny that the leisure class of the modern industrial state supplies any standard of good manners. On the contrary, as the elder aristocrats themselves deplore, one of the specific evils of the modern capitalist community, with its apotheosis of profit-making, on the one hand, and of luxurious idleness on the other, is a degradation of manners, more pernicious because more exemplary, than the coarse brutalities of the slum.

The Effect of Loss of Function

It is interesting to notice that, in the history of the world, the class of persons who were, by the coercive utilization of other people's labor, themselves relieved from industrial toil, had originally their own distinctive social function, other than that of "existing beautifully." They hunted for the food of the tribe; they fought in its defense; they performed the priestly offices on which its well-being seemed to depend; in Greece they were the philosophers and artists, in Republican Rome the statesmen and the jurists, and often the conquerors or administrators of subject-peoples. It has been reserved for the century of capitalism to produce an extensive class of persons, absolved from productive work, of whom a large proportion of the men, and nearly all the women, have no specific function, and disclaim the obligation of any social service whatever. We have already commented on the degradation of manners and morals, and the subtle corruption of other people's manners and morals, which is involved in the existence of a functionless rich class. But there is another cause for the deterioration, among the wealthy families in our modern societies of advanced capitalism, of what used to be counted as the social graces of a leisure class. These social graces went best, it will be admitted, with such aristocracies as those of the Court of Louis the Fourteenth, the old landed families of Carolina or Virginia, or the Samurai of Japan, the very essence of whose lives was a personal abstention from the conscious pursuit of pecuniary gain, and the maintenance of a rigidly defined caste system. It is evident, however, that such a division of activities cannot endure, because it has no root in nature. If the capitalist class would breed true to feudalism by producing only statesmen or soldiers, sportsmen or dilettanti, a stable medieval inequality might be maintained.   But Nature takes no notice of capitalism.   Statesmen and dilettanti are as rare among its scions as they are in the class which produced Wolsey and Richelieu.   Its energetic spirits have for the most part vulgar ambitions, vulgar capacities, and vulgar tastes in excitement.   They are competitive rather than coöperative: they like success, which means money-making and the personal power and prestige that money-making leads to; and the gambling element in big business flavors it attractively for them.   The specially active men arising in the old families nowadays vie with the crowd of the newly enriched in the making of profit by the organization and administration of the instruments of production.   This influence becomes, even in the richest circles, all-pervasive.   The " leisure class " of to-day, in Britain and France, no less than in America and Australia—far from being above and beyond the pursuit of pecuniary gain—is dominated by the desire for amassing more wealth, without any very nice discrimination between the different forms of production and the various kinds of profit-making that the law permits.   There is no longer an aristocracy, a bourgeoisie, and a working class.   There is a plutocracy and a proletariat; and it is in the proletariat that the old distinctions survive as ideals, and are miserably aped in practice; whilst in the plutocracy the big shopkeeper dines with the viscount, and all are rich tradesmen together.

The outcome of the attempt to combine the aristocratic ideal of a leisured class with the bourgeois pursuit of pecuniary gain is a state of manners which—at least to our taste—is unlovely to the last degree.[1] The ostentation of leisure, the choice of conspicuous and futile expenditure, the estimation of everything by its price, the measured appreciation of every person according, not to his quality or his achievements, but to his wealth, the consequent uncertainty as to everybody's " social position," the sycophancy towards millionaires, the almost irresistible arrogance given by the consciousness of possessions, and the subtle insolence that is involved in the conception that other persons with whom you habitually consort are social inferiors

[1] As has been pointed out by Veblen, the aristocratic or barbarian idea of a governing class depended on complete abstinence, not only from manual labor, but more especially from the brainworking process of profit-making, whether in manufactures, commerce or speculation. If the aristocrat was idle and luxurious, he was at least free from the active pursuit of gain. On the other hand, Werner Sombart shows that the old bourgeois ideal of a governing class is seen at its best in the early stages of capitalism when idleness and extravagance are the two deadly sins, and personal industry and personal thrift are exalted as the holiest of moral virtues. " 'Take as your model the ants,' wrote the father of Leonardo da Vinci (1339)—the most eminent bourgeois of his time—'who to-day already have a care for the needs of the morrow. Be thrifty and moderate'" (*The Quintessence of Capitalism,* by Werner Sombart, 1915, p. 111). Benjamin Franklin—the founder of the American bourgeois ideal—writes: " 'In order to secure my credit and character as a tradesman, I took care not only to be in reality industrious and frugal, but to avoid the appearance to the contrary. I dressed plain, and was seen at no places of idle diversion: I never went out a-fishing or shooting'" (*ibid.,* pp. 123-4). The leisure class of modern capitalism has lost the good and retained the bad features of both the aristocratic and the bourgeois ideals.

—all these characteristics of the society of all capitalist countries appear to us to reduce to an absurdity the claim that, in the present capitalist civilization, it is upon the existence of a leisured class that good manners depend.

THE EMERGENCE OF REALLY GOOD MANNERS

The socialist does not restrict himself to this negative criticism. He believes that a new conception of what is "good manners" is emerging in the modern democratic state, as an outcome of its democracy. When a definite system of social castes ceases to be maintainable, and social intercourse necessarily becomes general and promiscuous—as in the common membership of democratically elected bodies, or in the common use by all classes of the omnibus, the tramway, the American railway car, and now the British "third class" compartment—there is only one alternative to bad manners, and that is the common standard of mutual courtesy. This, in fact, constitutes the good manners of the remoter parts of contemporary Japan, where the nobleman or the millionaire uses the same ceremonious politeness to the porters as these do to him, and the great landlord to every one of his hundreds of peasant cultivators of rice and radishes, as his tenants themselves employ to the superior that they recognize. A similar extension of the conception of mutuality in a humane courtesy lies at the root of the typical "civilization" or urbanity in which modern France, owing to the traditions of the Revolution, is seen to excel, let us say, the Prussia of 1871-1918. It will be remembered that, already in 1879, Matthew Arnold took, for the text of his criticism of both the aristocracy of birth and the aristocracy of wealth of the Britain of his time, "a striking maxim, not alien certainly to the language of the Christian religion, but which has not passed into our copybooks: 'Choose equality and flee greed.'"[1] With Matthew Arnold, socialists believe in "choosing equality" as the essential element in good manners.

This fundamental condition of good manners was accepted by those who have, from time to time, been recognized as exemplars in the matter; but only as regards such as were admitted to membership of their own particular social caste. At all times, in well-mannered sets, all who were in the set have been expected, in social intercourse, to treat each other as equals. Already we extend this conception of social equality to the dinner table. We do not, when there is only just enough of anything to go round, seek to take for ourselves more than an equal share. We do not, nowadays, think it compatible with the manners of a gentleman to give the governess a cheaper wine than is served to the other persons at table, nor even

[1] "Equality," by Matthew Arnold, in *Mixed Essays,* 1879.

to put off the servants' hall with inferior meat. But towards the great unknown mass of our fellow-citizens, *who are really sitting down with us to eat at the world's table,* this principle of good manners is observed only by a tiny minority, even among those who think themselves well-bred. And this again is inevitable, because Nature still obstinately refuses to coöperate by making the rich people innately superior to the poor people. It is quite easy for the natural aristocrat to be exquisitely courteous to poorer mortals. His privilege is not challenged: the common man is touched by his condescension and eager to show that he knows how to respect genuine worth—that, as he phrases it, he knows a gentleman when he sees one. But the rich are not born with this natural superiority: they are in the lump as other men are; and their upbringing in comparative luxury tends to make them petulant, and expect a precedence to which their characters do not entitle them. Having no natural superiority, they are forced to assert their artificial privilege by insolence, and to demonstrate their power by expenditure. Without such insolence and such expenditure, they might as well be their own parlor-maids and butlers, who are often better looking and better mannered, and indeed could hardly obtain good situations if they were not.

Under such conditions it is useless to preach good manners and reasonable economy to people who combine average character with exceptional riches, not to

mention those who are below the average, and are born
mean, loutish, selfish, stupid, as happens just as often
to those who count their incomes in thousands as in
shillings. Bad manners become, if not literally compulsory, at least practically inevitable; and as in each
class the accepted standard of manners is simply what
everybody habitually does in that class, the great majority of people come to think it no more a breach of
good manners to be insolent and extravagant than to
spend and consume, by themselves and their families,
and thus to abstract from the world, just whatever income the accident of fortune gives them, irrespective
of whether or not the consumption is necessary for the
fullest performance of their duty to the community.

What stands in the way of the universal adoption of
the democratic conception of good manners in the
United States as well as in the Britain of to-day is,
in fact, the inequality of material circumstances and
personal freedom among the families, which are, in our
modern promiscuity of intercourse, driven into personal contact. It is for this reason that the best manners are to be observed—we venture to record what is
our own opinion—not in the " Upper Ten Thousand "
of Britain or the " Four Hundred " of New York,
but in certain strata of society where a practical equality of material circumstances happens to prevail, and
where social position depends on quite other circumstances than relative possessions. We may instance

the academic families resident in university centers, the still surviving skilled handicraftsmen of old-fashioned vocations, and the ministers of religion in denominations which have remained poor and lowly. The socialist contention is that, if we are to be gentlemen, not only must we intuitively refrain from taking more than our equal share of the good things of life, but we must also embody, in our social institutions, and especially in the way in which we collectively allocate among the whole of our fellow-countrymen the means of civilized life, that fundamental maxim, " choose equality and flee greed."

THE DYSGENIC INFLUENCE

There remains yet another indictment of the social stratification resulting from the inequality of personal riches, and the dominance given to it in capitalist society. Mr. Bernard Shaw, who more than any other socialist has brought into prominence both the evils resulting from disparity of personal riches and the ideal of equality of income as a fundamental part of the socialist creed, has given expression to this indictment in a characteristically challenging form. " I do not believe," he says, that " you will ever have any improvement in the human race until you greatly widen the area of possible sexual selection; until you make it as wide as the numbers of the community make it. Just consider what occurs at the present time. I walk down Oxford Street, let me say, as a young man. I see a woman who takes my fancy. I fall in love with her. It would seem very sensible, in an intelligent community, that I should take off my hat and say to this lady: 'Will you excuse me; but you attract me very strongly, and if you are not already engaged, would you mind taking my name and address and considering whether you would care to marry me?' Now I have no such chance at present. Probably when I meet that woman, she is either a charwoman, and I cannot marry her, or else she is a duchess, and she will not marry me. I have purposely taken the charwoman and the duchess; but we cut matters much finer than that. We cut our little class distinctions, all founded upon inequality of income, so narrow and so small that I have time and again said in English audiences of all classes throughout the kingdom 'You know perfectly well that when it came to your turn to be married, you had not, as a young man or a young woman, the choice practically of all the unmarried young people of your own age in our forty million population to choose from. You had at the outside a choice of two or three; and you did not like any of them very particularly as compared to the one you might have chosen, if you had had a larger choice.' That is a fact which you gentlemen with your knowledge of life cannot deny. The result is that you have, instead of a natural evolutionary sexual

selection, a class selection which is really a money selection. Is it to be wondered at that you have an inferior
and miserable breed under such circumstances? I believe that this goes home more to the people than any
other argument I can bring forward. I have impressed
audiences with that argument who were entirely unable
to grasp the economic argument in the way you are able
to grasp it, and who were indifferent to the political
arguments. I say, therefore, that if all the other arguments did not exist, the fact that equality of income
would have the effect of making the entire community
intermarriageable from one end to the other, and would
practically give a young man and young woman his or
her own choice right through the population—I say that
that argument only, with the results which would be
likely to accrue in the improvement of the race, would
carry the day." [1]

We may perhaps differ in the present state of our
knowledge of eugenics as to the weight to be given to
this plea for perfect freedom of sexual selection according to momentary impulse. But we must remember
that, a generation before Mr. Bernard Shaw, it had been
pretty conclusively demonstrated by Francis Galton that
the introduction of the motive of pecuniary gain—what
Mr. Bernard Shaw calls "money selection"—resulted

[1] "The Case for Equality," a lecture delivered at the National
Liberal Club, London; reported in *The Metropolitan* (New
York), December, 1913, and also published in London in pam-
phlet form.

in the progressive sterilization of the most promising stocks.

" MONEY SELECTION "

To Francis Galton's statistical demonstration of the socially disadvantageous consequences of the preference for heiresses of the most successful men of each generation, we may now add the adverse influence upon the birth-rate of the selection by the French peasantry, and generally by the petite bourgeoisie, of an only daughter as the wife for an only son, in order to accumulate the petty inheritances. In Britain and the United States we see this as the tendency to "marrying in," among wealthy families, in order to " keep the money in the family." Akin to this is the very common preference by parents who are keenly alive to their daughters' pecuniary advantage for sons-in-law of superior means, even with the drawbacks of age, weak health, lack of will-power, or deficiency in mental attainments. We see this deflection of sexual selection in its gravest form when the search for a husband or a wife endowed with the desired fortune leads, in circles high and low, to the acceptance of some one who is physically disqualified for healthy marriage, and even the morally degenerate, or the feeble-minded. The obverse of this " money selection," in all its forms, which no one can believe to be other than eugenically disadvantageous, is the intensification, among the least provident and most casual

of all classes, notably in the poorest stratum of irregu-
larly employed laborers of our great cities (who are to
a large extent condemned to a perpetual interbreeding),
of a reckless propagation that may well be eugenically
as adverse in its consequences to the community as the
exceptional restriction of the birth-rate among the
provident and the prudent.

The reaction of money selection on politics must be
treated separately; but we may quote here the epigram
made by Stuart Glennie at the expense of a gentleman
who obtained the means of entering parliament by
marrying the daughter of a rich manufacturer. He
described him as " M.P. by sexual selection." The
gentleman, as it happened, justified his success at the
poll; but that entirely accidental fact does not diminish
the intensity of the flashlight thrown by the sarcasm on
the power of inequality of income to corrupt the House
of Commons, which contains not a few " members by
sexual selection," and in like manner the whole system
of representative government.

CHAPTER III

INEQUALITY IN PERSONAL FREEDOM

THERE is another inequality in the capitalist state, which is perhaps more intensely resented by the modern artisan, and is more difficult to bring to the comprehension of the governing class than the inequality of income; namely, the disparity in personal freedom. Freedom is, of course, an elusive term, with various and conflicting meanings. To some simple minds freedom appears only a negation of slavery. To them any one is free who is not the chattel of some other person. The shipwrecked mariner on a barren island and the destitute vagrant wandering among property owners protected by an all-powerful police, are " free men," seeing that they " call no man master." But this sort of freedom is little more than freedom to die. In the modern industrial community, in which no man is able to produce for himself all that he needs for life, personal freedom is necessarily bound up with the ability to obtain commodities and services produced by other persons. Translated into the terms of daily life, personal freedom means, in fact, the power of the individual to buy sufficient food, shelter and clothing to keep his body in good health, and to gain access to sufficient teaching and books to develop his mind from its infantile state. Moreover, as we cannot regard as a free man any one with none but vegetative experiences, freedom involves the command at some time, of at least some money to spend on holidays and travel, on social intercourse and recreation, on placing one's self in a position to enjoy nature and art. We can, in fact, best define personal freedom as the possession of opportunity to develop our faculties and satisfy our desires. Professor Graham Wallas suggests the definition of "the possibility of continuous initiative." In this sense freedom is a relative term. It is only the very rich man who has freedom to consume all that he desires of the services and commodities produced by other persons, and also the freedom to abstain from all personal toil that would stand in the way of his "continuous initiative," and stop it by absorbing his energy and his time. Any poor man has a very limited freedom. To the propertyless wage-earner freedom may mean nothing more than the freedom, by dint of perpetual toil, to continue to exist on the very brink of starvation. Hence inequality in income in itself entails inequality in personal freedom.

"Equal Before the Law"

We have grown so accustomed, under the reign of capitalism, to the grossest disparity in personal freedom among nominally free citizens, that we fail to recognize

how gross and how cruel is the inequality even where
we profess to have adopted equality as a principle.
Both Britain and America are proud of having made all
men equal before the law.   Yet no one can even ask
for justice in the law-courts without paying fees which
(though the statesmen and the wealthy refuse to credit
the fact) do, in actual practice, prevent the great mass
of the population from obtaining legal redress for the
wrongs that are constantly being done to them.   The
very object with which the legal tribunals are established is to give men security for their personal freedom
—to prevent this being impaired by assaults, thefts, ex-
tortions, defalcations and failure to fulfill contracts and
pay debts.   In every city of Britain and America the
vast majority of the population never appear as plain-
tiffs in the civil courts, not because they are not as-
saulted and robbed, cheated and denied payment of
what is due to them—every one must know that these
evils happen much more frequently and, at one time or
another, much nearer universally, to the poor and
friendless than to the rich—but because they cannot
afford, out of their scanty earnings, even the court fee,
let alone that of the lawyer.   But the disparity in personal freedom between the rich and the poor is seen
most glaringly when the one and the other are charged
in the criminal court with an offense against the law.
The rich man, except in extreme cases such as murder,
practically always receives a summons; the poor man

is still often, for the same offense, peremptorily arrested, as was formerly always the case, and taken to prison to await trial. On a remand, the rich man easily procures bail, whilst quite a large proportion of propertyless defendants find themselves returned to the prison cells, a procedure which, coupled with their lack of means, does not, to say the least, facilitate their hunting up of witnesses who might prove their innocence, or their obtaining help in their defense. It is needless to recount the further advantages of the rich man in engaging the ablest lawyers and expert witnesses; in obtaining a change of venue, and successive remands, or in dragging the case from court to court. When sentence is imposed, it is, in the vast majority of cases, a pecuniary fine, which means practically nothing to the rich man, while to the poor man it may spell ruin for himself, his little business and his household. To the average police magistrate or clerk to the justices, it is quite a matter of course that a positive majority of those whom they sentence to small fines go to prison for one, two or six weeks, in default of payment. Ruinous as prison is known to be to the family of the prisoner as well as to the prisoner himself, the poor are sent to prison, in the United States as in Britain, by thousands every year, merely because they cannot immediately produce the few shillings or dollars that they are fined for minor offenses, which rich men commit daily with practical impunity. No inequality in personal freedom could be more scandalous than this practical inequality of rich and poor before the law courts, which characterizes every capitalist community, and which, though known to every judge and every practicing lawyer for a century, has remained unredressed.[1]

THE PSYCHOLOGICAL REACTION

But all this springs directly from the disparity in incomes, a material interpretation of personal freedom which does not exhaust the question. There is a psychological aspect of personal freedom which arises merely from the relation between one man and another. Even when the wage-earner is getting what he calls "good money" and steady work, he resents the fact that he, like the machine with which he works, is bought as an instrument of production; *that his daily life is dealt with as a means to another's end.* Why should he and his class always obey orders, and another, and a much smaller class, always give them? It is this concentration of the function of command in one individual, or in one class, with the correlative concentration of the obligation to obey in other individuals of another class, which constitutes the deepest chasm between the nation of the rich and the nation of the poor. In one of his novels Mr. Galsworthy vividly describes the contrast between the daily life of the English country

[1] See *The Law and the Poor,* by E. A. Parry, 1914.

house and the daily life of the laborer's cottage. The
rich man, and his wife and children, get up in the morning at any time they please; they eat what they like;
they "work" and they play when they like and how
they like; their whole day is controlled by the
promptings of their own instinct or impulse, or is
determined by their own reason or will. From morning till night they are perpetually doing what is pleasant
to them. They fulfill their personality, and they exercise what Professor Graham Wallas rightly calls their
"continuous initiative," by giving, day in day out, year
in year out, orders to other people. The laborer and
his family are always obeying orders; getting up by
order, working by order, in the way they are ordered,
leaving off work by order, occupying one cottage rather
than another by order of the farmer, being ejected from
home by order of the landowner, attending school by
order, sometimes even going to church by order; relying for medical attendance on the "order" of the Poor
Law Relieving Officer, and in some cases ordered into
the workhouse to end a life which, under the British
Constitution, has always been legally and politically that
of a freeman. From morning till night—save in rare
hours of "expansion" usually expiated painfully—the
"working class" find themselves doing what is irksome
or unpleasant to them. What is called in Britain the
governing class (which includes a great many more persons than are engaged in political government), is, typi-

cally, the class that passes its life in giving orders. What are called the "lower classes" are those that live by obeying orders.

WHEN AUTHORITY IS ACCEPTABLE

Now let no one imagine that these lower classes, or the socialists who champion them, or indeed any persons with common sense, object to one man exercising authority over another. What is resented in the capitalist organization of industry is both the number and the kind of the orders given by the rich to the poor, by the owners of land and capital to the persons who gain their livelihood by using these instruments of production. The authority of the capitalist and the landlord has invidious characteristics. It is continuous over the lives of the individuals who are ordered; it is irresponsible and cannot be called to account; it is not in any way reciprocal; it does not involve the selection of the person in command for his capacity to exercise authority either wisely or in the public interest: above all, it is designed to promote, not the good of the whole community, but the personal pleasure or private gain of the person who gives the order. No one but an anarchist objects to the authority of the policeman regulating the traffic in the crowded street; to the authority of the sanitary inspector compelling the occupier of the house to connect his domestic pipe with the main drain; to the

authority of the Medical Officer of Health enforcing
the isolation of an infectious person; or even to the
demand note of the tax-collector. No one resents the
commands of the railway guard—"take your seats"
or "all change here." All these orders are given in
respect of particular occasions in the citizen's life, and
by persons assumed to be selected for their fitness for
the duty of giving these particular orders. The persons exercising command are themselves under orders;
they are responsible to superior authority; and they
may be called to account for bad manners or for "exceeding their powers." Moreover, their orders are, in
the best sense, disinterested, and have no connection
with their personal gain or convenience. We may
complain that the official is going beyond his function
or is unmannerly in his methods. We may object to
the policy of the national executive, or deplore the
legislation enacted by Parliament. But in obeying
these orders all men are equal before the law; and all
men have the same right of appeal to the superior
authority. Finally, in political democracy, the persons
who are subject to the authority are exactly the persons
who have created it; and they can, if and when they
choose, sweep it away. In their capacity of citizen-
electors they may exercise collectively, through the
Parliament and the government of the day, an ultimate control over the stream of orders they are called
upon as individuals to obey.

In this connection it is interesting to notice the socialist interpretation of a phrase much in vogue in the twentieth century. We often hear at labor meetings of the desirability of a man " controlling his own working life." But this does not mean that each man or woman is to be free to work at starvation wages, or for excessive hours, or under the most unpleasant conditions. This is the freedom demanded for the worker by the capitalist. Against it the socialists and the organized workers have carried on a war of attrition for a century, the victories in that war being factory laws, mines and railways regulation laws, minimum wage laws, and the like. What the insurgent worker means by " the worker's control over his own life " is, on the contrary, the sort of control exercised by means of his trade union, through an executive council and officials, whom he and his fellows have elected, and can depose. These agents of the workers stand or fall, paradoxical as it may sound to those who still ignorantly regard trade unions as tyrannies, according to their ability to maintain and increase the personal freedom of the persons who elect them. The revolt of the workers is not against authority as such, but against the continuous and irresponsible authority of the profit-making employer. Where is the warrant, he asks, for the power of the owners of factories and mines, land and machinery, to dictate the daily life and the weekly expenditure of hundreds of their fellowmen, and even, at their pleasure, to withdraw from them the means of life itself? This power is not derived from popular election. It has no relation to the ascertained merit or capacity of those who wield it. It is, in many cases, not even accompanied by any consciousness of responsibility for the moral or material well-being of those over whom it is exercised. Not only is there no necessary connection between the particular orders which the workers find themselves compelled to obey, and the security or prosperity of the commonwealth: there is often a great and patent contradiction, orders to adulterate and cheat being quite common. From the standpoint of labor the authority of the capitalist and landlord is used for a corrupt end—to promote the pecuniary gain of the person in command.

DICTATION AS TO ENVIRONMENT

Few persons who have not deliberately analyzed the way in which the wage-system is organized have any adequate conception of the continuity and the dictatorial character of the stream of orders by which the workman is called upon to direct his life. But this stream of orders is not the only way in which the property-owning class directs the daily life of those who are dependent on their toil. Even more dangerous, because more subtle, and less obviously an outcome of the inequality in wealth, is the power possessed by the propertied class to determine, for many years at a stretch, what shall be the physical and mental environment, not only of the manual laborer, but of all the local inhabitants. The most striking manifestation of this power is the steadily increasing " industrializing " of a countryside, ending in the creation of an urban slum area, by the continuous pollution of the water and the atmosphere, the destruction of vegetation, the creation of nuisances, the erection of " back to back " dwellings, in row after row of mean streets. The devastation wrought in this way, in some of the most fertile and most beautiful parts of England and Scotland, as also in the United States, is, as we now know, comparable only to that effected by a long-drawn-out modern war. In peace times the community as a whole fails to realize, in time, the catastrophe that is being caused by the private ownership of land and capital in the establishment and growth of an industrial center. By the time that the evil is recognized, the health and happiness of whole generations have been vitally affected. Belated statutes and tardy by-laws may then, at best, lessen the pollution, abate the darkening of the atmosphere by noxious gases and coal smoke, perhaps even save the last surviving vegetation. But nothing can bring back the lives the dictatorship of the capitalist has wasted. The leisured rich are able to escape from the

noise, the gloom, the dirt, the smoke, the smells that
their power has created; but the wage-earners, the
industrial brain-workers, and all their retinue of professional men and shopkeepers find themselves compelled to dwell, and to rear their families, in the grace-
less conditions unconsciously determined for them by
the industrial and financial organizers in their pursuit
of private gain.   When the city dweller escapes into
the still unspoilt countryside on a scanty holiday, it
comes as a new insult to find himself and his children
barred from the pleasant park, excluded from the
forest, and warned off the mountain and the moor by
the property rights of the very class of persons who
have rendered his place of abode abhorrent to him.   In
the end he is forced in self-defense to form a perverse
habit of liking grimy streets, blackened skies, and the
deafening clatter of drayhorses' shoes on stone sets,
on the principle that if you cannot have what you like
you must like what you have.

DICTATION OF THE MENTAL ENVIRONMENT

Nor is even this unconscious determination by the
property-owning class of the material environment of
the mass of the community, for the sake of its own
private gain, the worst form taken by the inequality in
personal freedom.   It has been reserved to our own
time for the profit-making capitalist to determine also

the mental environment. Who can estimate the effect on the mind of the incessantly reiterated advertisements that hem us in on every side? It is, moreover, the capitalist who directs the character of the recreation afforded to the mass of people. It is the brewery company and the distillery that give us the public house; other capitalists, controlling the music hall and the cinematograph, may say, with Fletcher of Saltoun, that they care not who makes the laws as long as they provide the songs and films. But the most glaring instance of the capitalist direction of our mentality, and perhaps, ultimately, the most pernicious, is the modern system of ownership of the newspaper press. Here we have even a double capitalist control, first by the millionaire proprietors of whole series of journals, daily, weekly, and monthly under autocratic control, and secondly, by the great dispensers of lucrative advertisements to these journals. The combination of the colossal expense involved in the successful conduct of a modern daily newspaper, and the natural reluctance of the wealthy advertisers to support any publication adverse to the system, if not even to the particular business, by which they obtain their own fortunes, have made it almost impossible for the propertyless wage-earners, even in coöperation with each other, to establish, either in Britain or the United States, any organ of their own at all comparable in circulation and influence with those of the millionaire proprietors.

Thus, the mass of the population is quite unable to protect itself against the stream of suggestion, biased information, and corruptly selected news that is poured on them by the giant circulation of the press.[1]

Lastly, we have the control insidiously exercised by the owners and organizers of the instruments of production, by means of their wealth, over the working of municipal government and parliamentary institutions.

DICTATION IN GOVERNMENT

Of this control, the direct power of the proprietors of the newspaper press—which, in Britain, goes far to make a Prime Minister, and in the United States not only to elect a President but also to go far to select his chief ministers—is only the most obvious example. The influence, not only upon elections and legislatures, but also upon national and municipal executives, of the great financial, shipping, manufacturing, and trading amalgamations and combinations, in which the power

[1] For accounts of the manner and extent to which the newspaper press, and behind it the possessors of wealth, now control the mental environment, as well as the local and central government of the United States and Britain, the student should consult *The Press and the Organization of Society,* by Norman Angell, 1922; and *Liberty and the News,* 1920, and *Public Opinion,* 1922, both by Walter Lippman, himself the editor of a great New York newspaper; the more lurid descriptions given from personal experience as journalists, on the one hand, by Hilaire Belloc in *The Free Press,* 1918, and by Upton Sinclair in *The Brass Check,* 1919; and, incidentally, in the technical account of how a modern newspaper is run, by G. B. Dibblee in *The Newspaper,* 1913 (London), and by John La P. Given in *Making a Newspaper,* 1913 (New York).

of wealth is cast defiantly into the scale as the sword of Brennus, has, in recent decades, become notorious and scandalous. It is, we suggest, to the suspicion, followed by the detection of this far-reaching coercive guidance of national and local government by the property-owners and profit-makers, large and small, more than to any other cause, that is to be ascribed the sudden and rapid decay of the confidence of the wage-earning class in these institutions, manifested not in this country alone, but throughout the Continent of Europe and North America. Unfortunately, one invidious feature of the Great War, so far as the United Kingdom is concerned, has been the extension of a similar capitalist control to the national executive, in ways not previously open. The temporary handing over of various government departments to leading representatives of the business interests concerned, and the shameless use of the influence thus acquired for the promotion of the private profits of those branches of business, represents, so it is felt by the British workman, the final degradation of the state to be the handmaid and accomplice of the profiteer.

THE BRAIN-WORKERS IN CAPITALIST SERVICE

This control of the physical and mental environment, which, in a capitalist society, the property-owning class progressively and almost automatically accomplishes (for all those effects are mere incidents in the pursuit of private gain, and are no more consciously aimed at than the devastation caused by the trampling of a herd in pursuit of food), brings into prominence the instrument of its far-reaching dominance. The deep-seated intolerance by the more ignorant manual workers of the very existence of the professional brain-workers is not due solely to the difficulty a navvy finds in believing that a man who sits in a comfortable chair by a cheerful fire in a carefully sound-proofed room is doing any work at all, much less work that will leave him hungry and exhausted in three or four hours. Many wage-workers are sufficiently educated to know better; and others are employed in occupations quite as sedentary and even less apparently active than those of the financier or mathematician. Their share in the prejudice is explained, if not justified, by the fact that the brain-workers, in every capitalist state, find themselves attracted, and economically compelled, to take service under the property-owners. Historically the professions emerge as the hirelings of the governing class for the time being. In the modern industrial system they naturally serve the proprietors of the instruments of production, who alone can insure to the vast majority of them a secure and ample livelihood, with some prospect of climbing up to the eminence of "living by owning." The lawyers, the engineers, the architects, the men of financial and administrative ability, the civil servants, the authors and journalists, the teachers of the schools beyond the elementary grade, the whole class of managers, the inventors, even the artists and the men of science—not altogether excluding, in spite of their long charitable service of the poor, the medical profession and the ministers of religion, nor yet, for all their devotion to the children of the masses, even the elementary school teachers— are almost inevitably retained, consciously or unconsciously, in the maintenance and defense of the existing social order, in which the private ownership of the instruments of production is the corner-stone. Is it surprising that the manual workers of the world should be tempted to regard, not science, art or religion (as is often ignorantly asserted), but the brain-workers who have been trained under the capitalist system, and enlisted in its service, as being as much the " enemies of the people " as the " idle rich "? But this is not all. The brain-workers themselves, especially those who are poorly paid and socially segregated, are beginning to rebel openly against this all-pervading coercive guidance of national policy and national culture by wealthy men and a wealthy class. As school teachers, as municipal officials, as civil servants, as scientific workers, as journalists and editors, sometimes even (notably in the United States as under the German Empire) as university lecturers and professors, they find their freedom of thought and expression strangled by the fear of dismissal, or at any rate by that of losing all chance of promotion, should they dare to oppose not merely the political party or the pecuniary interests of influential patrons, but even the current principles of social organizations to which nearly all rich men cling. Moreover, the majority of the situations of authority and affluence are still habitually reserved, in most countries, either by administrative devices or through personal influence, for persons who have qualified as brain-workers though belonging to the class of those who live by owning or organizing the instruments of production, irrespective of their inferiority of attainments or inability to render, in the posts to which they are assigned, the highest service to the community. It is here that we find the fundamental cause of the prevailing unrest in all countries in practically all the brain-working professions, leading in many cases to the adherence of the younger professionals to the socialist movement, and nowadays even inclining some of the professional organizations to make common cause with the trade unions and the labor and socialist parties in resisting the dominance of the property-owners.

WHY LIBERALISM DECAYED

We may suggest that the foregoing analysis incidentally reveals the root-cause of the universal failure of the political parties styled Liberal, which were so typical of the advanced thought of European nations during the nineteenth century—notably at the zenith of unrestrained capitalism—to retain, in the twentieth century, their hold of a wage-earning class that has become conscious of its citizenship. To the political Liberals, personal freedom actually meant the personal power of the man of property; just as political progress meant the abolition of feudal, ecclesiastical and syndicalist restrictions upon the right of the property-owner, small as well as large, to do what he liked " with his own "—his own land and capital no less than his own personality. Down to the present day the unrepentant Liberal refuses to recognize—cannot even be made to understand—that, in the modern industrial state, a man who is divorced from the instruments of production cannot, as we have shown, even live his own life, let alone do what he likes with his own personality. Even to the political Liberal who is not a capitalist, such as the young barrister or doctor, artist or author, the conception that the laborers' engagement for hire is of the nature of " wage-slavery " is unintelligible. To him it seems, on the contrary, that the typical engagement for hire of the propertyless professional, " calling no man master " but earning his livelihood by fees from a succession of clients, upon no one of whom is he specially dependent, constitutes the very perfection of honorable service which is perfect freedom. What even this highly educated Liberal fails to understand is that, whatever may once have been the case, the industrial revolution has made anything like the freedom of professional life impossible for the artisan or the factory operative, the laborer or the clerk. The fact that the ordinary manual worker or minor clerical employee has not the ownership, and, therefore, not the control of the instruments of production, or of the complicated industrial or financial organization by which he can earn a livelihood, and cannot support himself on a succession of fees from a multitude of clients, compels him, whether or not he desires this, to obtain his food by placing himself under a master whom he cannot call to account; whose orders he has to obey; whose interests he has to serve; who, in fact, possesses him and uses him, during the greater part of his waking life, for ends which are not his own. He cannot choose where he will live, and in what environment his children will grow up. He finds himself restricted in the amusements and even in the literature to which he has access, to that which it suits the pecuniary interests of the capitalist class to supply. He finds, as it seems to him, nearly every professional brain-worker retained against him and his class. And through this control over his working life and his leisure hours, over his physical and mental environment, the propertyless worker, by hand or by brain—though conscious that he and his fellows constitute a majority of the electorate—discover that even with the widest suffrage he is unable, in fact, to control the government of his state. Accordingly, once he has been admitted to voting citizenship, the liberty which Liberalism offers him seems a hypocritical pretense. He finds in the creed of Liberalism no comprehension either of the nature of the servitude in which the capitalist system has engulfed the great bulk of every industrial community, or of the need for an application to industrial organization of the first principles of democracy. Now this comprehension is the very atmosphere of socialism. The socialist is out to destroy the dictatorship of the capitalist. And as that dictatorship is the grievance which the worker is never allowed to forget for a single working day from his cradle to his grave he naturally turns to socialism the moment he begins to connect politics with his personal affairs and perceives that his vote is an instrument of political power.

A LIBERAL APOLOGY FOR CAPITALISM

The honest defenders of capitalism admit, in substance, the truth of this criticism; but they allege, in reply, that without the potent stimulus of private profit it would have been impossible to have effected the Industrial Revolution, or to have secured the vast increase in the production of commodities and services, on which, it is suggested, modern civilization depends.

It was not merely that there was, even in the foremost nations, between the seventeenth and the nineteenth century, no practicable alternative to the dictatorship of the capitalist. The very inequality in riches and in personal freedom, by the prospect of which he was incited and stimulated, seemed to have an economic advantage of its own which obscured its social drawbacks. As it has been well put by a contemporary economist, in the course of the nineteenth century, " Europe was so organized socially and economically as to secure the maximum accumulation of capital. While there was some continuous improvement in the daily conditions of life of the mass of the population, society was so framed as to throw a great part of the increased income into the control of the class least likely to consume it. The new rich of the nineteenth century were not brought up to large expenditures, and preferred the power which investment gave them to the pleasures of immediate consumption. In fact, it was precisely the *inequality* of the distribution of wealth which made possible those vast accumulations of fixed wealth and of capital improvements which distinguished that age from all others. Herein lay, in fact, the main justification of the capitalist system. If the rich had spent their new wealth on their own enjoyments, the world would long ago have found such a régime intolerable. But like bees they saved and accumulated, not less to the advantage of the whole community because they themselves held narrower ends in prospect.

"The immense accumulations of fixed capital which, to the great benefit of mankind, were built up during the half century before the war, could never have come about in a society where wealth was divided equitably. The railways of the world, which that age built as a monument to posterity, were, not less than the pyramids of Egypt, the work of labor which was not free to consume in immediate enjoyment the full equivalent of its efforts.

"Thus this remarkable system depended for its growth on a double bluff or deception. On the one hand the laboring classes accepted from ignorance or powerlessness, or were compelled, persuaded, or cajoled by custom, convention, authority, and the well-established order of society into accepting, a situation in which they could call their own very little of the cake, that they and nature and the capitalists were co-operating to produce. And on the other hand the capitalist classes were allowed to call the best part of the cake theirs and were theoretically free to consume it, on the tacit underlying condition that they consumed very little of it in practice. The duty of "saving" became nine-tenths of virtue, and the growth of the cake the object of true religion. There grew round the non-consumption of the cake all those instincts of puritanism which in other ages has withdrawn itself from the world and has neglected the arts of production as well as those of enjoyment. And so the cake increased; but to what end was not clearly contemplated." [1]

We need not demur to this candidly realistic *apologia* for nineteenth century capitalism. Of course it was not the whole, or even the bulk of their vast share of the national income that the capitalist classes abstained from consuming year by year, in order to transform it into new instruments of wealth production; but only a fraction of their share—in the United Kingdom of the nineteenth century, scarcely a quarter of it! And of this quarter, how much was invested in instruments for the production of what Ruskin called illth, of gluttony, extravagance, waste and demoralization? For, under capitalism, wealth is counted in a false currency. But it may be freely admitted that, with all its drawbacks, the dictatorship of the capitalist scored an initial success. It delivered the goods. It created the highly efficient machinery of ever-increasing production. And, gruesome as were the accompanying social results, we may, perhaps, allow that, on balance, down to a certain date, the advantages exceeded the drawbacks. With this initial success we deal in the next chapter.

[1] *The Economic Consequences of the Peace*, by John M. Keynes, 1920, pp. 16-17.

CHAPTER IV

THE INITIAL SUCCESS OF THE CAPITALIST SYSTEM

WE can imagine the impatience of some of our readers with the foregoing description of the evils accompanying modern industrialism. The enlightened upholder of capitalistic business enterprise will accuse us of the common fallacy of the agitator—the fallacy of concentrating attention on the black patches of an existing order, without taking account, either of its achievements, or of the fact that all qualities and all successes must have their defects and their shortcomings. The philosophical adherent of the dictatorship of the capitalist profit-maker will have felt that our criticisms center round what he may admit to be a regrettably unequal distribution of wealth, and an unscientific consumption of commodities and services. But he will retort that commodities and services have first to be produced. It is fair to argue that the poverty of the poor, the inequalities within capitalist communities in incomes and in personal freedom, the control over the environment and the coercive guidance of national policy exercised by the capitalist because of his status and his wealth, in so far as these are

78

evils at all, are only incidental to a greater good; [1] that
they may possibly be remediable by appropriate re-

[1] It may be noted that the most skillful defenders of capitalist
civilization argue in defense of the gains of the entrepreneur,
organizer or director of industry; tacitly ignoring the tribute
that mere ownership levies in rent and interest, and quietly
assuming the very point at issue, by implying that in no other
way than by extending the conception of private property to
the instruments of production, can the services of the entrepreneur, organizer or director be obtained. Thus, an able American defender of the capitalist system remarks that "land, capital and labor are only productive factors in the sense of being
the means by which those who assume the direction and responsibility of industry carry on production. The entrepreneur or
enterpriser is the only real productive factor. Pure rent, pure
interest, and pure wages are what the enterpriser has to pay to
obtain the privilege of controlling and utilizing these three
means. . . . Just as there would be no advantage to the human
body in diverting blood from the brain to some other part that
receives only one-tenth as much blood as the brain, so there
would result a loss rather than a gain from any such equaliza-
tion of income as would deprive the more efficient members of
society of the incentive to the utmost exercise of their productive power, or of the ability to fit themselves for, and perform
successfully, the important duties that devolve upon them as the
undertakers of enterprises, the discoverers and appropriators of
opportunities, and the accumulators of capital" (*Enterprise and
the Productive Process*, by Fred B. Hawley, 1907, pp. 85, 122-3).

"Profit is acknowledged to be a peculiar form of income,
differing essentially from rent, wages, or interest, and entitled to
rank with them as a fundamental form of equal, but only equal,
theoretic importances. It is also identified with the 'residue of
the product,' after the fixed claims of land, labor, and capital are
satisfied. And it is looked upon as the income peculiar to the
entrepreneur, who is regarded as 'the coördinator of land,
capital and labor, without furnishing either in his own capacity.
. . . The peculiar function of the economic entrepreneur is the
assumption of responsibility in industrial undertakings. . . .
Strictly speaking, a coördinator is not only the one who plans,
but also the one who intelligently executes a plan, and the two
may be, and usually are, different persons. The executant, in
carrying out the original plan, has to adjust details, and this
involves a certain amount of subsidiary planning on his part,
but his function in the economic productive process is universally recognized as labor, and the income obtained by him
as wages. . . . It is only when the coördinator subjects himself

forms within the capitalist system; but that in any case they are of trifling account in comparison with the benefit the community derives from the enormous increase in national wealth and national power directly attributable to the business enterprise of the capitalist profit-maker. To such a person what seems essential is the organization of the instruments of production in the manner that is continuously the most efficient in maximizing output. This continuous increase in the production of commodities and services is, it is claimed, what distinguishes a progressive from a stagnant or a decadent civilization. Such a continuous advance of wealth production, in quantity, quality, and variety, can be achieved, it is assumed, only by evoking in men continuous initiative, industry, persistence, courageous adventure and thrift, for which the one known stimulus is pecuniary gain; by securing to them unfettered freedom of enterprise, subject to the check of personal loss of wealth whenever they fail, for which there is only one known expedient: namely,

to the result of his own coördination, or of the coördination of others, that he becomes the recipient of profit. . . . If the coordinator should be exclusively defined as the one who subjects himself to the results of coördination, the person at whose risk and for whose benefit coördination is effected, it would be synonymous with the term 'enterpriser' as I have employed it" (ibid., pp. 11-13).

This, however, leaves undefended what John Stuart Mill described (Principles of Political Economy, p. 477 of edition of 1865) as the "enormous share which the possessors of the instruments of industry are able to take from the produce," in the rent and interest payable to functionless shareholders and landlords.

THE NATURE OF PROFIT-MAKING

private ownership of the instruments of production united with their organization and administration.

THE CORE OF THE CASE

We shall not understand the clash of views, nor do justice to the position on each side, unless we realize that in this controversy the defenders of the capitalist system and the labor and socialist movement of the twentieth century join issue on the very core of the case. The modern controversy between the believers in a new order of social democracy and the most enlightened adherents of the capitalist system turns, in fact, on the efficacy or indispensability of the motive of profit-making and its defects; upon the relative advantages and disadvantages, to the community as a whole, of leaving the control of the nation's land, machinery, labor and brains to the profit-making manufacturer, merchant or financier.

THE NATURE OF PROFIT-MAKING

What is profit-making, and what is the vocation of the profit-maker?

According to the economists, profit-making satisfies " a certain propensity in human nature, the propensity to truck, barter and exchange one thing for another." It is a natural development from the higgling that takes place in the primitive market between individual producers of different commodities or services. The producer of one article seeks, by the art of bargaining, not only to exchange the surplus of the commodity which he himself makes, for a commodity which he desires but is unable to produce, but to exchange it to the greatest advantage to himself so as to get the product of more labor for the product of less labor.[1] As Adam Smith rightly observes, the art of bargaining is a distinct advance on the animal's art of seizing without giving anything in return. " Nobody ever saw one animal," he writes, " by its gestures and natural cries, signifying to another ' this is mine, that yours: I am willing to give this for that.' " The dog seizes

[1] In an address to Japanese students Sir Rabindranath Tagore gives us the criticism of an Eastern philosopher of Western commercialism. "You had your own industry in Japan; how scrupulously honest and true it was, you can see by its products —by their grace and strength, their conscientiousness in details, where they can hardly be observed. But the tidal wave of false-hood has swept over your land from that part of the world where business is business, and honesty is followed merely as the best policy. Have you never felt shame when you see the trade advertisements, not only plastering the whole town with lies and exaggerations, but invading the green fields, where the peasants do their honest labor, and the hill-tops, which greet the first pure light of the morning? . . . This commercialism with its barbarity of ugly decorations is a terrible menace to all humanity, because it is setting up the ideal of power over that of perfection. It is making the cult of self-seeking exult in its naked shamelessness. . . . Its movements are violent, its noise is discordantly loud. It is carrying its own damnation because it is trampling into distortion the humanity upon which it stands. It is strenuously turning out money at the cost of happiness. . . . The vital ambition of the preseent civilization of Europe is to have the exclusive possession of the devil" (*Nationalism,* pp. 85-86, 129, 128, 82).

the bone from the other dog and runs away with it.
The Western tourist, observing the chaffering of an
Eastern bazaar, has some difficulty in distinguishing
the art of bargaining from the art of cheating, that
is to say the art of getting something for nothing by
false pretenses and fraud, and not by force. The distinction seems to be more a matter of degree than of
kind. The famous Hindu poet-philosopher of our
own day, surveying the larger transactions of the capitalist profit-maker in the money, stock, produce and
labor markets of Western civilization, finds a similar
" stop in his mind." [1]

The transaction of the capitalist profit-maker is distinguished from the bartering between individual producers by the fact that he exchanges the product, not
merely or mainly of his own activity, but of that of
countless other persons. Hence he conducts a double
transaction: he first buys the labor, or the product of
the labor, of other persons at the cheapest rate, and
then sells the resultant commodity or service at the
highest price. It is exactly this element in capitalist
enterprise which is termed the " exploitation of labor," or, more recently, " profiteering." The capitalist's profit is found, essentially, in the margin between
the price he gives for other men's services and the
price which he gets in selling the product of these

[1] " The foremost truth of political economy," observes Nassau
Senior, is " that every one desires to obtain individual wealth
with as little sacrifice as possible."

services in the markets of the world.   The capitalist profit-maker may (and usually does) add to the function of profit-making some other function, such as that of organizing and sometimes directing the technical processes of agriculture, mining, manufacture, transport, banking, warehousing, or shop-keeping.   But all these services can be and are increasingly performed, notably in the fully developed capitalist system, by salaried professionals who are not themselves profit-makers, but merely wage-laborers of a high grade, having no personal interest in the margin obtained between the act of buying and the act of selling.

How Profit-making Arose

Now we must always remember that profit-making as a method of remunerating the directors of industry and commerce, was not adopted out of malice.   It was not intended to produce masses of destitute persons. It was not designed to diminish personal freedom and to lead to class oppression.   It was not even devised for the creation of an hereditary class which lives by owning.   The economic institutions necessary to the vocation of profit-making—private property in the instruments of production, and free enterprise in the use of such instruments—were maintained and developed by British and American statesmen and legislators during the eighteenth and nineteenth centuries, with the approval of the economists, because these men honestly believed that unrestricted profit-making by manufacturers, traders and financiers was the most effective way of increasing the national wealth.[1] There has never been, at any period of British history, a more unanimous verdict from the most intelligent and public-spirited leaders and instructors of the governing class than that which acclaimed the industrial revolution of the eighteenth and nineteenth centuries. The most learned philosophers, the most progressive politicians, the most enlightened authors, all repeated in their different ways the following series of dogmatic propositions, which semed to them to constitute a train of reasoning, and which have, in the United States, become so axiomatic as to be taken habitually for granted. The happiness of the community depends on its wealth; the wealth of the nation depends on maintaining and increasing its annual product; the best way of doing this is by letting each citizen make himself as rich as he can in his own way; the quickest way to personal

[1] "The institutions of private property and individual competition are based, not on blind traditionalism or class oppression but on the experience which all the progessive races of mankind have attained of their social utility and their flexible adaptability to changing social needs" (*Socialism: A Critical Analysis*, by O. D. Skelton, 1911, p. 45). Note the inability or unwillingness to distinguish between "private property" and "private property in the instruments of production." Paradoxical as it may seem, one of the principal objects of the socialist is greatly to increase the amount of "private property," but to concentrate it entirely on the forms of wealth for which the institution is fitting. (See *A Constitution for the Socialist Commonwealth of Great Britain*, by S. and B. Webb, 1920, pp. 340-47.)

riches is profit-making in a free market; hence unrestricted profit-making by individual capitalists is the best way of securing the welfare and happiness of the nation.[1]

This plea of the capitalist had, at the time it was formulated, much to be said for it. Even to-day socialists are apt to ignore the cogency of the argument for the profit-maker as a factor in the production of wealth, and to concentrate their attack on the assumption that the welfare and happiness of the nation depends on an actual increase of the national product. Confronted with the actual results of the capitalist organization of industry in all parts of the world and under all conditions—the poverty of the poor and the gross inequality which it creates in " life, liberty and the pursuit of happiness "—the socialist finds it easy to argue that the welfare of a community depends only to a small extent on the amount of its annual product, and much more on the efficient distribution and efficient consumption of such commodities and services as are produced. There are, indeed, some socialists who have gone so far as to deny that any increase of productivity is required for an increase in human happi-

---

[1] " The question is still the same, ' How to make the nation as rich " as possible," ' but as the answer now is ' By letting each member of it make himself as rich as he can in his own way,' that portion of the old art of Political Economy which professed to teach a statesman how to ' provide a plentiful revenue or subsistence for the people' becomes almost evanescent " (*The Principles of Political Economy*, by H. Sidgwick, 1883, p. 18).

ness. They maintain that the present national product
of Britain or France, Australia or the United States,
if equally distributed and efficiently consumed, is amply
sufficient to secure all the consumption that is good for
all the inhabitants of those countries. This is not our
own view of the situation.

The Efficacy of the Profit-making Motive

We think the present output of commodities and
services, relatively to the efforts and sacrifices of those
who coöperate in production, is disastrously small;
and that, assuming that there is no overwork, and sufficient leisure for full citizenship, every increase in the
production of commodities and services may mean, if
fairly distributed and efficiently consumed, additional
personal freedom for each individual citizen, as well as
a progressive improvement of the race. But the socialist, when he asserts that increased productivity is
not necessary or even desirable, is not squarely meeting the case against him. The capitalist retorts that,
unless the organizers of industry are remunerated by
the process of profit-making, and permitted to enjoy
all the advantages that this involves, even the existing
wealth of the nation will not be maintained; and that
it may easily be so much diminished, and so rapidly,
that the whole community will promptly come to the
very brink of starvation. " Inequalities in wealth,"

sums up an American critic of socialism, " which correspond to differences in enterprise, in industry, in thrift, can be leveled only at the cost of paralyzing production, and plunging the whole of society into an equality of misery." [1] " The making of profit," we are told by a great British capitalist, " decides whether labor has been wisely applied or material rightly used. Men will not pay for what they do not want, nor on the other hand continue to supply that by which they gain nothing. Thus we have in profit the final economic justification of expenditure in trade. Every transaction comes to be tried in the court of profit or loss, and no business enterprise, unless it be experimental or educational or philanthropic in its character, which does not respond to this guidance can be permanently either successful or useful." [2]

No competent observer of the business world will deny the efficacy of profit-making as a way of stimulating and canalizing the energies of those who practice it. Uncertainty as to the end to be pursued is perhaps the commonest cause of paralysis of will; it leads both to delay in the execution, and to a wavering uncertainty as to the direction of a given undertaking. We may admit that pecuniary gain—the fact of finding more money in your pocket at the conclusion than at the opening of a transaction—is an end that is under-

[1] *Socialism: A Critical Analysis,* by O. D. Skelton, p. 58.
[2] *Life and Labor of the People in London,* by Charles Booth, second series; " Industry," vol. 5, 1903, p. 77.

stood by practically all human beings.[1]   The motive of
pecuniary gain is vividly felt by the common run of
men; it is usually present, sometimes abnormally present, in the make-up of mental defectives and degen-
erates, and it may even be discovered in many popular artists and some men of science.   Further, in the
profession of profit-making, the test of success is iden-
tical with the end pursued.   The successful profit-
maker who becomes a millionaire adds, to his personal
satisfaction with every increase of his gains, the high
reputation which he comes to enjoy, exactly because
of his wealth, among his fellow business men.
"Good" business means big profits; "bad" business
means small profits; whilst bankruptcy spells disgrace,
however innocently it may have been incurred.[2]   We

[1] "The beginning and the end of capitalist economic activities
is a sum of money.   Consequently, calculation forms an important element in the capitalist spirit, and this was recognized quite
early in the history of capitalism.   By calculation I mean the
tendency, the habit, perhaps more—the capacity, to think of the
universe in terms of figures, and to transform these figures into
a well-knit system of income and expenditure.   The figures, I
need hardly add, always express a value; and the whole system
is intended to demonstrate whether a plus or a minus is the
resultant, thus showing whether the undertaking is likely to
bring profit or loss" (The Quintessence of Capitalism, by
Werner Sombart, 1915, p. 125).
[2] "When do we speak of having accomplished a successful
piece of business?   Surely when the contract-making has ended
well.   But what is meant precisely by 'well'?   It certainly has
no reference to the quality or to the quantity of the goods or
services given or received; it refers solely and only to the return
of the sum of money expended, and to a surplus over and above
it (profit).   It is the aim of the undertaker so to manipulate the
factors over which he has control as to bring about this surplus" (The Jews and Modern Capitalism, by Werner Sombart,
1913, p. 161).

realize the truth of this analysis when we compare the business world with that of the learned professions. The great lawyer, the great surgeon or physician, or the great civil engineer may derive the most solid of his secret satisfactions from the magnitude of his income and the growth of his fortune. But among the members of his own profession his prestige will rest, not on the size of his banking account, but on the quality of his work, whether as counsel or as judge; in diagnosis or in treatment; in the complexity or the importance of the enterprise that he has engineered. It is exactly this simplicity and uniformity of the end pursued, and its acceptance by public opinion as the test of success, which transforms the profit-maker from a puzzled human being, grappling with ever new ends or aims, into an automaton working without friction on a repetition job. But this is not all. The process of profit-making calls to its aid all the more primitive and commoner passions of men: the instinct of acquisition, the instinct of fighting or domineering over other men, the instinct of obtaining for wife and children a position of security or privilege. Moreover, the combination of the process of profit-making with the law of inheritance brings into play one of the strongest of all civilized instincts: the desire to " found a family ": that is, to secure to one's descendants the right for all time to live by owning, and thus be independent of the need for ability or industry. The adherents of the capitalist system are therefore justified in asserting that the process of profit-making is a sort of alchemy for getting the largest output in the way of continuous and concentrated effort from even the dullest intellect and the meanest character that can be brought into its crucible. No vocation that has ever existed has been so absorbing and so transforming to the man who practices it. All the common instincts, impulses and faculties of the " average sensual man " are, to use an American expression, " routed " to a given end. Through the intense concentration of the whole of their thought and feeling on this one narrow issue, men who would not otherwise be distinguished become prophets and seers, and develop an almost animal " smell of the market " which enables them to foretell with amazing exactitude what transactions, in all types of enterprise, among all races and throughout all continents, will, as they say, " pay." There is probably no efficiency so great as the efficiency of the successful profit-maker. Of all specialists he is the most perfect.

In justice to Adam Smith and his immediate followers, it is worth remembering that the efficacy of the process of profit-making was far greater in the first stages of the capitalist system than it is to-day. For a very good reason. Before the rise of joint-stock enterprise on a huge scale, still more before the rise of the modern amalgamation and trust, the profit-maker

was a free agent, a man who called no man master.
He was able to act quickly without waiting for the
decision of any other mind. If he failed in intelligence or character he alone had himself to thank, and
he knew it. If he succeeded, all the profits were his,
and all the prestige. He worked day in and day out
with this consciousness of the hell of penury on one
side, and the paradise of huge possessions on the other.
If we think of the life of the modern manager of the
joint-stock bank or railway company, or the salaried
agent of the typical world-wide trust, with his subordination to a board of directors, his obligation to
fulfill his prescribed function according to definite rules
laid down for him by Company Acts, by auditors' requirements, by the technique of whole series of experts, by arrangements with allied or amalgamated
companies; and on the other hand, secured in his salary,
and bearing none of the loss of failure, always able to
leave one company and go to another, one realizes the
superior incentive to the brain-worker, and the superior
freedom of the entrepreneur, of the period of industrial revolution to that of established and developed
capitalism.

To " Get Rich Quickly "

Thus, we must admit the accuracy of one among
the series of propositions constituting the plea of the

capitalist: namely, "that the quickest way to personal riches is profit-making." To which we may add that it is a way that is open to all, whether they be Fords or Fledgebys, who can pursue it single-mindedly, and are not so "unbusinesslike" as to allow themselves to be distracted by unselfish interests. And the efficiency of profit-making as a means to an end—a hard fact for the socialist—is proved, not only by observing the characteristics of the profit-maker, but also by the statistical result of the process. Those nations which have adopted the capitalist organization of industry in its most complete form have both the richest individuals and the largest class of persons who are rich enough to live by owning and not by working. If personal riches be the test of national wealth we are a long step forward towards accepting the plea of the capitalist.

But the profit-maker does not work in a vacuum. He is made by and he makes the political, social and economic environment in which he functions. It is to the character of this environment that we must now turn our attention.

The Capitalist Environment

There is no more fascinating historical study than to trace the emergence of a new type of human being in response to new circumstances; to watch the individuals of this incipient subspecies coalesce into a group with the common purpose of self-preservation against hostile conservative forces. If the group is successful in its defensive phase it presently becomes openly aggressive. Recognized as a reputable profession, it seeks to alter social and political institutions so as to give fresh scope for the exercise of the new vocation. For instance, we see the present medical profession in Great Britain originating in the humble apothecaries' and barber-surgeons' shops of medieval times; working in the seventeenth and eighteenth centuries through chartered colleges and companies towards corporate influence as a self-governing profession; gradually entrenching itself in the hospital system of the last quarter of the eighteenth century, and reaching its present position through the Medical Act and the General Medical Council of 1858, consolidated by the ever-widening development of public health and physical education, of medical registration and national insurance. To-day, it is not too much to say, the medical profession in Great Britain, relatively insignificant in numbers, exercises greater power in the machinery of administration and the counsels of the legislature than even the formally established Anglican Church: rivaling the equally influential legal profession in its implicit claim to direct the destinies of the community and the race.

The Coming of the Capitalist

But the rise to power of the medical profession—perhaps because it has not been accompanied, taking the profession as a whole, by any considerable acquisition of personal wealth—exhibits none of the revolutionary romance and political glamour, the mass and the momentum, of the rise, during the eighteenth and nineteenth centuries, of the class of capitalist entrepreneurs to a position of predominance in the modern industrial state. The unlicensed profit-maker, or " new capitalist," appears first as the rebel of his time, flying the flag of personal freedom as the arch-destroyer of existing conventions, institutions and creeds. The reason for his revolutionary fervor is plain. The vocation of the profit-maker, as we have already described, is always to buy in the cheapest and to sell in the dearest market. Clearly, his first requirement is free access to markets at home and abroad, whether for the purchase of raw materials, the hiring of labor, or the sale of his product. At the beginning of the eighteenth century in England, this freedom of enterprise was hampered and barred in all directions. Hence the incipient class of capitalist profit-makers, aided by their allies in Parliament, in the university lecture-room and in the press, proceeded ruthlessly to smash up the existing social institutions that stood in their way. We see them smashing up the Tudor and Stuart regulation of wages and prices; smashing up the manor, its courts and its common-fields; smashing up the chartered national companies with their monopolies of mining and manufacturing, or of foreign trade and overseas jurisdiction; smashing up the municipal corporations with their gilds, their systems of apprenticeship, and their prohibition of trade by the " foreigner " (who was only the immigrant from the next town or the adjacent countryside); smashing up the old Poor Law with its archaic system of settlement and its stagnant pools of rate-aided under-employed laborers; smashing up the home and the family, with its immemorial domestic manufactures, in order to scatter its members, women as well as men, children as well as adults, in the new factories in distant counties. They even smashed up, in 1832, the British Parliament, based on the pocket-boroughs of the Crown and the feudal lords, and the obsolete vocational franchise of the ancient municipalities.   In fact the capitalist entrepreneurs were, for the better part of two centuries, the Bolshevists of their time, believing—to use the famous words of the petition of the Liverpool merchants of 1834—" that all *in equal station* should enjoy equal privileges," [1] and rigidly excluding from participation in the government of the country the propertyless wage-earners who were driven into their

---

[1] *The Manor and the Borough*, by S. and B. Webb, 1908, p. 701.

employment.   It is, indeed, scarcely too much to say that the government of Great Britain between 1799 and 1832, intoxicated by the growth of national wealth under the new capitalism, established a reign of terror over the manual workers.   " The employers' law," to quote the historians of the working-class of these years, " was to be the public law.   Workmen were to obey their master as they would obey the state, and the state was to enforce the master's commands as it would its own.   This was the new policy behind the Combination Laws of 1799 and 1800.   These two Acts, the second modifying the first, prohibiting all common action in defense of their common interests by workmen, remain the most unqualified surrender of the state to the discretion of a class in the history of England." [1]   One only of the ancient institutions of the realm the capitalist oligarchy clung to and developed: the law of private property, with its adjunct in legally protected inheritance of wealth by the living from the dead.

The Ruthlessness of Capitalist Destruction

It is worth notice that the insurgent capitalist entrepreneurs, in the century of their exuberance, were in another respect analogous to Bakunin, the Anarchist,

---

[1] *The Town Labourer, 1760-1832*, by J. L. and Barbara Hammond, 1917, p. 113.

and Lenin, the Communist, who in the Russia of 1918-1919 had the opportunity of putting in practice so much of the spirit of Bakunin's teaching.   They were absolutely ruthless in the clearance that they made of everything that stood in the way of the carrying out of their ideas of social reorganization—neither weighing in the balance the incidental advantages of the system that they considered obsolete, nor heeding the suffering that their revolution caused to individuals without number—and, what should never be forgotten, making no compensation whatsoever for the breach of legally "established expectations" to the uncounted multitude of innocent persons whose incomes were annihilated and whose very livelihood was destroyed by the revolution that they brought about.   The craftsman who had gained his qualification by apprenticeship; the laborer who had a statutory right to be "set to work" by the Overseers of the Poor in the parish in which he possessed a legal settlement; the little copyholder relying on his immemorial right of common pasture; the freeman of the ancient Municipal Corporation, who had a legal right to be protected against the "foreigner"; the member of the Craft Gild, enjoying a corporate monopoly of the trade, all enjoyed legally established vested interests, which formed as validly part of their personal estates as the forests and steppes of the Russian noble, and the factories and shops of the Russian "bourgeoisie." [1] To the British capitalist entrepreneurs of 1750-1850, as to the Russian Bolshevists of 1918-19, all these "legalisms" seemed but obsolete wreckage impeding the inauguration of a more profitable (or, as they chose to consider it, a more equitable) social order.

THE ACHIEVEMENTS OF THE CAPITALIST

Much is subsequently forgiven to a revolution which succeeds; or which, to the active spirits of the rising generation, appears to satisfy the national needs. It is therefore worth inquiring whether the dictatorship of the capitalist, which, in Britain, came to its zenith in the middle of the nineteenth century, fulfilled any wider purpose than its immediate one of enriching the proprietary class. We may say at once that, in our opinion, this dictatorship of the capitalist did, on the balance, in spite of the atrocious debit account for which Ruskin coined the word "illth," more good than evil; at any rate, from the latter part of the

---

[1] To the peasant cultivator and master craftsman, "the original idea, essence and purpose of property"—to quote an American writer—"was to secure to a person or group of persons the use and control of the things which that person or group needed for his or its own subsistence and welfare" (*American Socialism*, by James Mackaye, pp. 34-5). To the individual producer of the pre-capitalist era, owning his instruments of production and pursuing his own vocation, the Industrial Revolution seemed wholly inconsistent with the rights of property, not only as he understood them, but also as they had been interpreted by Common Law and local custom from time immemorial.

eighteenth to about the middle of the nineteenth century. During the latter part of the nineteenth century its success, on balance, was doubtful; and in the twentieth century, even in respect of the increase in national figures (we purposely, like Ruskin, hesitate to use the word " wealth "), its drawbacks outweigh its advantages.

There can be no doubt that, in the Britain of the latter part of the eighteenth and the beginning of the nineteenth century there was a sudden, an enormous and a continuous increase in production and productivity, whether measured in the quantity and range of the generally useful commodities consumed or in the amount of plant made available for their production. The very increase in population, which was so marked a feature of this period, in contrast with any previous century, and which was itself a direct result of the dislocation of domestic agriculture and manufacture, represented a great growth of productive power. The continuous expansion of the imports of raw materials and of the exports of manufactured goods meant a widening of the range and an increase in the amount of the consumable commodities that constituted the nation's income.

THE INCREASE IN PRODUCTION

The extension of British trade to all countries, the growth of British shipping, the rise of British banking and insurance, in a world in which British capitalists found themselves in a position of commercial dominance with the very minimum of foreign competition, all coöperated to produce a golden stream of almost boundless profits, taking the form of constantly swelling incomes for the capitalist class, a heaping up of all the accompaniments of luxurious living, and a perpetual investment of the surplus in additional instruments of wealth production, from the sinking of more mines and the erection of new factories to the launching of ships, the building of railways, the multiplication of machinery and the opening up of ever-widening markets. And this unprecedented increase in production is not demonstrated only by the statistics. We can trace every stage in the process. The passing away of domestic manufacture and peasant cultivation, together with the silent abandonment of the habit of "living in" by the farm laborer, and the massing of individual factory operatives in crowded urban slums, produced a reckless unrestrained breeding, which placed at the capitalist's disposal a rapidly increasing and economically defenseless labor force. The autocratic power of those who could offer, in wages for the new processes, practically the only available means of subsistence, almost automatically set each man, woman and child to the tasks for which they were best fitted, for the longest possible hours, in return for the lowest possible wages. Presently, the substitution, for the laxity of the old Poor Law, of the ruthlessly deterrent workhouse system brought actual hunger to the fortifying of the power of the employer, and made the entry into his service as compulsory as it would have been under direct industrial conscription. If we think of human beings as merely instruments of production, there can be no hesitation in ascribing to the capitalist organization of Britain, at its most glorious period, an unprecedented success, in harnessing to production the greatest amount of labor-power at the least relative cost in maintenance, a success demonstrably superior to that of the most efficient system of chattel slavery and the slave trade that the world has known. Moreover, the capitalist system evoked and utilized a great increase of mental as well as of manual productivity. The shattering of the old order opened a career to acquisitively inventive brains of every grade and enlisted them in the new industrial organization. There were endless opportunities made for the capable and adventurous. Large numbers of craftsmen and peasants escaped from the common fate of being pressed down by under-employment and declining earnings to become foremen and managers, and eventually independent capitalist entrepreneurs. It may well be that it was at this period that the largest number and the greatest proportion of persons rose from the lower ranks into the governing class. The stimulus was as great as the opportunities were numerous; and if the selection was in some respects dysgenic, it was concentrated on the one quality of ability to increase production and diminish its cost.   It was, above all, an age of mechanical contrivance, in which an unprecedented amount of mental energy was put into improving industrial processes.   And the demand for commodities was boundless.   The whole world was hungering for the textile fabrics, the hardware, the porcelain, the arms and ammunition, the clothing, the leather goods, that were being produced by the new processes at ever lower prices.   Meanwhile the British manufacturers themselves were insatiable in their demand for ever-increasing quantities of raw materials from the ends of the earth to convert into the commodities of which the other countries seemed never to have had enough.   The British profit-makers spent their days, not in devising means of competing successfully against each other, or with foreign rivals, but in coping with new demands; searching for new materials; creating new products; adventurously opening up new markets; risking fortune, and sometimes even life, in commercial ventures, from China to Peru, from the wilds of Western America to the primitive barbarism of the Antipodes.   The prizes were, of course, colossal.   " It was not five per cent or ten per cent," it has been observed, " but thousands per cent," that made the fortunes of the Britain of this glorious time.

It must, we repeat, be admitted that, despite all drawbacks, this enormous development of successful profit-making meant, at any rate for the time being, a vast increase in that part of the nation's earnings which may fairly be called its wealth. If wages were low, and the conditions of labor so bad as to be destructive of the people, the continual pressure for a cheapening of production—especially after the general removal of taxes upon commodities of common use—largely benefited the consumer. The profit-makers themselves found their greatest gains in increasing output and consumption by a continuous lowering of the price of commodities that every one consumed and of services that every one used. Combination among capitalists, in such a way as permanently to maintain prices above the cost of production, was practically unknown. The whole nation shared, through declining prices, combined with a reasonably stable currency and, on the whole, stable or even slightly rising rates of wages, in the ever-growing stream of commodities, and steadily widened the range and increased the quantity of its consumption.

To those who regard an immediate increase in national income as, if not the only, at least the main condition of social progress and well-being, it will seem fortunate that British capitalism for the time being attained its end, for there was, in the century of the Industrial Revolution, no available alternative. As has been remarked by Werner Sombart, " economic activities in the pre-capitalist period were regulated solely in accordance with the principle of a sufficiency for existence: and peasant and craftsman looked to their economic activities to provide them with their livelihood and nothing more."[1] The vast majority of these independent producers had no ambition to heap up riches. They raised their crops and made their wares largely for their own use; and their strongest impulse was to live their own life in their own way, working when they liked, sleeping when they liked, eating when they liked, and playing when they liked. The best of them were inspired, not by the desire for gain but by the instinct of workmanship. It must, however, always be remembered that, with regard to their surplus output, the peasant cultivator and the master craftsman were as truly "profit-makers," with the shortcomings and defects of the profit-maker, as the capitalist entrepreneur. In many cases they were themselves "exploiters" of other people's labor, of the labor of their apprentices and journeymen, and of their own families. Whatever may have been the virtues of such an order of society, it did not, as a matter of fact, develop either the large outlook or the self-control requisite for directing enterprise on a large scale. Nor did it produce either the spirit of association or the capacity for representative institutions, which lie together at

[1] *The Quintessence of Capitalism,* by Werner Sombart, 1915, p. 172.

the base of modern political and industrial democracy.[1]

THE ABSENCE OF ALTERNATIVE

Hence in the eighteenth and even in the early part
of the nineteenth century, no public or collectivist organization was practicable in Britain. There was no
supply of officials who were even moderately honest.
The records of central departments and of such contemporary local government as existed in Britain show
that it was impossible to get a class of civil servants
who did not take bribes, directly or indirectly, or who
could be depended on to do a day's work; whilst most
minor officials were addicted to drink and did not
scruple to steal the petty cash. Posts in the public
service were spoken of and asked for as sinecures.
There was no body of knowledge as to the processes
or methods of administration on a large scale, no way
of testing the abilities of the candidates for appointment, no system of professional training, so that every
public position was either hereditary or inevitably
jobbed, falling often to the least competent members of

[1] The incapacity for democratic institutions—for the trade
union or professional organization as well as for political democracy—is seen in the special liability to the disease of bureaucracy
of countries like Japan, Russia, and even modern France—the
explanation being, we think, that a community of individual producers is, through lack of large outlook and the capacity for
association, compelled to leave the government of such centralized institutions as are requisite in the modern world to a
hierarchy of officials, whom they are alike unable and unwilling
effectively to criticize and control.

the governing class. The nascent professions of mining, of civil and mechanical engineering, of industrial chemistry, of architecture and building construction, of administration itself, proceeded only by "rule of thumb" and "trial and error." There was no efficient bookkeeping, no system of audit, even in its rudimentary form of an audit of cash accounts; and the very idea of "costing" was undreamt of. The intensity of the motive of profit-making as a means of personal gain supplied the only stimulus and test by which men could be selected, processes invented, management conducted, methods cheapened and markets discovered. And the capitalist system had, incidentally, the merit of training the nation in the science and art of coöperative working in manufacture, transport, commerce and finance. Even its oppressions and its frauds had their uses, in that they drove the proletariat of manual-working wage-earners which capitalism created, to combine in trade unions and coöperative societies, and to develop their own faculties for free association and industrial representative institutions. Profit-making was, in fact, at the opening of the nineteenth century, the world's substitute for qualities which did not at the time exist, for self-discipline, for professional technique, for scientific knowledge, for public service, for the spirit of free association, for common honesty itself.

CHAPTER V

THE EVENTUAL FAILURE OF THE CAPITALIST SYSTEM

How long did it last, this initial success of the reign of capitalism?

It is, of course, impossible to assign to any one year the date at which capitalism, in all its manifold developments in agriculture, in mining, in manufacture, in finance and transport and trading at home and abroad, changed, in any particular country, from being a national advantage, to being, on balance, a national drawback. Moreover, there is a relative as well as an absolute efficiency; and it is of little use estimating the absolute efficacy of profit-making as a method of stimulating and remunerating industry before alternatives became available. Roughly, it was not until the middle of the nineteenth century that the more penetrating observers began to urge that the dictatorship of the capitalist had not only hopeless limitations in wealth production, but was actually producing a great deal that was the very reverse of wealth. From about that time onward, as is now evident, profit-making became increasingly subject to malignant growths and perverted metabolisms, which created their own poisons and lessened the advantages of the system itself. It is only within the past half-century that alternative methods of organizing industry, demonstrably superior in the equitable distribution and efficient consumption of wealth, and, as we should claim, all things considered equal, if not superior, in the production of wealth, have been discovered and applied.

The Adverse Developments of Capitalism

This failure of modern business enterprise can be traced to certain inherent defects in the motive of profit-making, and to certain inevitable developments in the profession of the profit-maker. We shall leave out of consideration such obvious anomalies as the interests created by capitalism in destruction by accident, catastrophe, and the utmost acceleration of wear and tear in all commodities. From the interest of the glazier in the hailstorm to the interest of the wayside garage in accidents to motor cars and of the huge railway wagon repairing industry in the most destructive and wasteful methods of transport, there are more examples to hand than we have room to describe, or even enumerate, of the fact that under capitalism it is impossible to create an interest in production that is not also an interest in decay and destruction. We therefore propose to describe this failure under the following heads only. The profit-maker is, by the nature of the case, led to damage and destroy, not only the most valuable of the instruments of production, but also some of those that are irreplaceable; he tends to adulterate (or to produce inferior substitutes for) necessary commodities; he often employs his own and other people's labor in producing commodities and services of no social value—sometimes, indeed, ruinously pernicious; and he is found eager to use his own and other people's capital and credit in ways productive of profit to himself, but of nothing else. Even in the early competitive stage of capitalism the simple fact that when the community wanted one pair of new boots a hundred boot manufacturers made a pair in the hope of catching that single customer caused industry to proceed in a series of gluts and depressions which were demoralizing personally and disastrous financially. Crises were as much a matter of course as cholera epidemics. But now that we have survived this phase, the perpetual pressure for increased output and larger transactions leads to periodical depressions in the markets of the world, which may even become chronic, with a consequent hypertrophy of the organization for sale as compared with the organization for production, so that, as is currently said, " it costs more to sell an article than it does to make it." Although within each country the principle of free competition among capitalist profit-makers, which was assumed to guarantee to the consumer the lowest price and the best quality, is superseded, in industry after industry, by combinations among capitalists to secure monopoly prices and to compel consumers to accept articles standardized in the interests of the profit-maker, the separate industries and combinations of industries, freed as they are from internal competition, are still driven fatalistically to compete with one another for the fresh capital that never ceases accumulating, and, when they get it, to launch into increased production to employ it and earn dividends on it, without regard to the demand for its products, which they accordingly must excite by all the arts of advertisement and commercial traveling, and all the political intrigues of the hunt for foreign markets, sometimes poetically called " places in the sun." Thus the desire to hold old markets and the greed to acquire new ones on the part of the capitalist manufacturer, trader and financier in each of the great European states, reveals itself as the fundamental cause of the catastrophic world war of 1914-18, with its twenty millions of dead, and its unexampled devastation of territory and destruction of wealth. Finally, the growing hatred of the capitalist dictatorship, and the increasing anger of the proletariat at the permanent inequality in income and personal freedom which the capitalist system entails, is culminating in a suicidal class war within each of the great industrial states.

THE DAMAGE AND DESTRUCTION OF THE INSTRU-
MENTS OF PRODUCTION BY CAPITALIST PROFIT-
MAKERS.

The first discoverer of this evil was the founder of
British socialism (Robert Owen), who insisted, at the
very beginning of the nineteenth century, that the capitalist system is ruinous in its effects on the instruments
of wealth production with which it works. Owen,
himself a capitalist, was the first of his class to understand that his instruments of production were, as Bismarck said of the instruments of diplomacy, blood and
iron, and that, as another famous German had pointed
out, "blood is a quite peculiar juice." Let us work
out his thesis.

All instruments of production except living ones
wear out by use; and, the faster they produce, the
sooner they are worn out. The capitalist employer has
therefore to solve two problems as to his tools and
machines. First, how much shall he allow in his yearly
balance sheet for their depreciation by wear and tear?
Second, as the wearing out of a machine may be described as working it to death, and as the length of
time occupied by the process varies with the speed at
which it is driven, what length of life can he most
profitably allot to it? The initial factor in the calculation is the cost of the machine. A savage, whose
hammer is a stone and whose lever a stick, costing him

only the trouble of picking them up, need not consider whether they will last him ten minutes or ten years: there are plenty more where they came from; so he may be as careless and destructive as he likes as far as they are concerned. But if he uses an implement which takes him a day to make, and wears it out or breaks it in half a day, he will be bankrupt and destitute before the end of the week. In the same way, if an employer pays £5000 for a machine, and wears it out before it has produced £300 worth of goods or services, the machine will ruin him instead of enriching him. On the other hand, if the machine is used so sparingly that it becomes obsolete before it has paid for its cost, or produces so slowly that the loss of time costs more than the wear and tear of working it harder, it will pay the employer to speed it up. It may be a delicate matter to ascertain the precise point at which the profit is greatest; but the delicacy is not sentimental: the feelings of the machine may be left out of account because it has none; and the interest of the community may be left out of account because it does not clash with that of the producer. And about scrapping the machine the moment a better one can be procured there is no compunction whatever.

But if the instrument of production is not a machine, but a living organism, the problem becomes sentimentally complicated at once. If the savage, instead of spending a day to make an implement, has to spend ten days catching a wild horse and breaking it in, and he proceeds to overwork, illtreat, and starve that horse to death before it has repaid the ten days' work with something to boot, then clearly he will share the horse's fate presently.   Like the employer with the machine he has to ascertain how long he should let the horse live in order to get the utmost profit out of him.   A slave-owner has to make the same calculation as to his slaves.   Such calculations are made quite cold-bloodedly as a matter of capitalistic business.   Before slavery was abolished in the southern States of North America it had become accepted on certain plantations that the most profitable system was to wear out the negroes in eight years.   Before horse traction had given way to electric traction for tramways in London, it was calculated that the greatest profit was made by using up the horses in four years.

Obviously the substitution of hired white labor for enslaved black labor, or the substitution of hired horses for owned horses by the tramway company, does not change the nature of the calculation.   When the Lancashire factory owners were reproached with using up nine generations of men in one generation, their reply, when they were imprudent enough to reply frankly, was that the calculation worked out that way whether they liked it or not, and that business is business.

Such calculations are not admissible in the interest of the community.   In spite of the political power of the employers, Parliament was forced by the atrocity of the results to intervene with Factory Acts, the beneficent effect of which, not only on the factory employees, but on the employers' profits, proved that the calculation had been not only inhuman but so ignorantly and inaccurately made that the employers had been led by it into killing the goose that laid the golden eggs. Nevertheless, the corrected calculation is as irreconcilable finally with human welfare as the inaccurate one. It is not possible to prove that a quite unrestrained and unscrupulous sacrifice of humane considerations to the single aim of attaining the maximum profit for each particular employer may not at any moment in any industry lead to higher dividends than those attained under the Factory Acts.

There is an economic as well as a vital difference between the mechanical and human instruments of production employed in capitalism. The capitalist has to pay the whole cost of the machine and even more, whilst the human instrument, though much more costly to produce, can be had for nothing. His mother's pains and risks and housekeeping, his father's labor, his education at the cost of the ratepayers, the common resources placed at his disposal by municipal and national Communism, the wastage of human life which goes with the successful survival of each able-bodied worker; all these are the prime cost of the man before he presents himself at the factory gate begging for a job; but the employer acquires him as an instrument of production for nothing, his only expense being the bare cost of maintaining his power of working from week to week by food, clothing and lodging, precisely as if he were acquiring a steam engine for nothing, and supplying it with oil and fuel at its own expense. If, by abusing this gratuitous living instrument of production by overdriving or underfeeding, he damages it, or uses it up so fast that it is " too old at forty," all he has to do is to throw it back into the street on to the hands of the ratepayer, and pick up a new human instrument on the same terms.

Against so outrageous an incentive to abuse and deterioration of the national human stock an individual may stand out here and there either by a self-impoverishing refusal to engage in business at all, or by a personal generosity supported by exceptional organizing powers in certain special departments of business; but capitalist employers as a class cannot stand out against it. Under its pressure we have not only what is called a submerged tenth of the population, but eight tenths who can barely keep their heads above very dirty water, the remaining tenth having to spend the resultant profits mostly in keeping out the sea of misery which surrounds them. It makes wholesale degradation of the nation inevitable, because four out of every five of its adult heads of families have no other means of livelihood than to sell themselves as instruments of production, and those to whom they sell themselves have no uncommercial interest in them, and no public responsibility for them. That such a system should endure as the basis of a high civilization is inconceivable. Just think of it. The colliery owner has to buy another pony for the one he kills in the mine, or do without it. He has not to buy another boy for the one that gets killed with the pony. The very next morning his agent finds at the gate another boy, or perhaps many other boys, standing, ready-made, to be taken on for weekly subsistence in the place of the one who has been killed. That is why the typical entrepreneur in all capitalist countries has remained so indifferent to the disease and death rate among the " hands " that he employs as, in the first instance, intuitively to oppose every measure introduced for their protection. But accidents are the least of the evils. We need not again recite the tragic story of abject poverty, brutal demoralization and premature death wrought among millions of families by the unrestrained capitalism of the first half of the nineteenth century, through underpayment and overwork, through the formation of stagnant pools of casual labor and the creation of recurrent periods of unemployment without wages. And let us not flatter ourselves that this is merely an incident of the past. The evils of low wages, long hours and insanitary conditions still drag on in every industry in which the dictatorship of the capitalist has not been limited by the authority of the law or the rival command of the trade union; whilst the slow starvation due to under-employment or unemployment is still only mitigated by costly and demoralizing doles at the public expense. This damage and destruction of the human instrument of production cannot be regarded as a mere perversion of the capitalist system. It is now seen to be an inevitable incident of the profit-making process itself. Indeed, in the final analysis it is obligatory on the individual profit-maker by the nature of his being; for unless in exploitation he keeps up with the most ruthless of his competitors, the very profit by which he lives, dependent as it is on the margin between cost and selling price, eventually disappears. By the end of the third quarter of the nineteenth century, this side of the failure of capitalism had become recognized by candid students all over the world.

A later discovery was the ruin which capitalism brought on those common resources which were not reduced to private ownership, such as the air which the profit-maker's industry contaminates with smoke and noxious fumes; the running streams which it pollutes; the thoroughfares and waste spaces which it befouls. Any respect for these common requisites of healthy existence is an impediment to individual profit-making, and hence under its dictatorship cannot be maintained. Who can measure the diminution in

health, in happiness, in morality and in intelligence—
all factors in human productivity—caused through the
profit-maker by the defilement of air, water and land,
and the destruction of all amenity and beauty in the
surroundings of countless millions of his fellow-
citizens?

THE RUIN OF NATURAL RESOURCES

Nor is it man and man's environment alone that the
profit-maker destroys: it is not only the older civilizations that he contaminates.   In pursuit of the limitless
natural wealth of new and slightly peopled lands the
profit-maker proceeds with his destructive process
from continent to continent.   Natural resources are
abundant and cheap: in many places they are costless.
Hence fur-bearing and food animals are killed, in season and out of season, to the point of extermination
of the species; primeval forests are leveled to the
ground; natural pastures are denuded; virgin soils are
defertilized; coal and metals, oils and gases—all reserves of potential power—are wasted and exhausted;
the rivers are dried up, and the very climate is impaired.   No one will accuse the government of the
United States of being anti-capitalist, or of having
any theoretical prejudice against the process of profit-
making.   But no Bolshevik agitator could denounce
the devastation and destruction of the natural resources
of the American continent, in more unmeasured terms

than President Roosevelt and the governors of the separate states have done. " I have asked you," gravely stated President Roosevelt to the conference of governors in 1908, " to come together now, because the enormous consumption of these resources, and the threat of imminent exhaustion of some of them, due to reckless and wasteful use, once more calls for common effort, common action. . . . It is equally clear that these resources are the final basis of national power and perpetuity.   Finally, it is ominously evident that these resources are in the course of rapid exhaustion." [1]   " To-day as you ride through the South," asserted Mr. J. J. Hill, one of the greatest of America's industrial magnates, " you see everywhere land gullied by torrential rains, red and yellow clay banks exposed where once were fertile fields, and agriculture reduced, because its main support has been washed away.   Millions of acres, in places to the extent of one-tenth of the entire arable area, have been so injured that no care can restore them." [2]   " There is no doubt," declared President James of the University of Illinois, " that we have in many directions wasted our patrimony.   In our haste to get rich we have overreached ourselves and undermined the very basis on which a permanent national industry and a permanent national life must

[1] *Proceedings of the Conference of Governors on the Conservation of Natural Resources,* May 13-15, 1908 (House Documents, vol. 128, No. 1425, 2nd Session, 1908-9, p. 67).
[2] *Ibid.,* p. 67.

rest." [1] " Prodigious waste has accompanied our use
of the forest," report the government experts. " The
chief causes are fire, wasteful methods of logging and
turpentining, waste in the mill, and waste in the use of
wood." [2] A similar tale of destruction is told about the
mineral products: " the percentage of coal left in the
ground beyond recovery," an American expert told
the conference of governors, " varies from 40 to 70
per cent in the different fields, to say nothing of the
wasteful and extravagant use of the portion extracted;
while the waste of natural gas, the most precious fuel
of all, is so vast that no one can even approximate the
percentage. . . . The forces of greed and selfishness
are so entrenched behind corporate power and influence that to attack them may often appear to you useless as the labors of Sisyphus; but as you love your

[1] *Ibid.*, p. 174.
[2] " The experience of half a century has clearly shown in
Virginia, the Carolinas and Georgia that turpentining under
present methods renders a permanent naval-stores industry in
the South utterly impossible. These methods usually render the
forest unproductive in four or five years. They have so greatly
reduced the long-leaf pine forests available for turpentining that
in some localities trees 4 or 5 inches in diameter are now being
boxed. This generally means an exceedingly low return in tur-
pentine and the death in a year or two of trees, which would
otherwise have grown to make lumber. . . . And year by year,
through careless cutting and fires, we lower the capacity of
existing forests to produce their like again, or totally destroy
them. . . . By wasteful logging, fire, and general failure to
provide for a second crop, we have made our forests less productive than any others of similar area in the world, in spite of
the remarkably quick growth of most of our timber trees " (*Report of the National Conservation Commission*, vol. i, Senate
Documents, vol. 10, No. 670; Sixtieth Congress, 1908-9, Statement
by the Secretary of Forests, pp. 57-9).

states and country, I adjure you to take up this fight for the conservation of our fuel resources with the determination never to surrender until the forces of greed and avarice which are so rapidly sapping the very foundations of our country's greatness capitulate, and agree to end the wild riot of destruction that has characterized the past." [1]   The capitalist in Canada is no better than the capitalist in the United States. " At Calgary just before the war," we are told, " they discovered petroleum in an indifferent quantity at a single well. Within forty-eight hours land in the neighborhood was changing hands at between £10,000 and £12,000 an acre, and companies had been floated with a capital of £12,000,000; concessions were being granted and leases signed at machine-gun speed; and even if a true oil-field had been revealed it would have been quickly drained and devastated by a mob of promiscuous, unregulated, competitive drillers." [2]   Once more we must emphasize the fact that the cause of all

[1] No. 1425, *Proceedings of the Conference of Governors on the Conservation of Natural Resources,* May 13-15, 1908 (House Documents, vol. 138), p. 36.

[2] *The Observer,* June 1, 1919. " That has been the history of almost every oilfield opened on the American continent," the writer adds. "A strike, a rush of speculators, a great boom in the price of land, indiscriminate drilling on plots so small that the derricks, as one catches sight of them, seem to be literally touching one another, a dozen wells sunk in an area that can barely support three, each frenzied small-holder drilling as fast as he can to prevent the oil beneath his plot of ground from being drained away by his neighbor and rival, no scientific precautions to conserve the gas which will alone force the flow of oil, a feverish higgledy-piggledy of cut-throat, beggar-my-neighbor competition, in the course of which anywhere from half to

this devastation and destruction is not the malice of
man, even of capitalist man, but the inevitable result of
profit-making enterprise. " Before the older states,"
summed up one of the governors, " realized the value
of their forests, their waterways, their mines and minerals, they had allowed all to slip from their hands and
into private ownership. The same thing is now going
on in the younger states; and soon there will be left
nothing to conserve of what we received from our fore-
fathers as a magnificent heritage." [1] " The pecuniary
demands of those directly interested and occupied in
such industry," explained a contemporary economist,
" be they promoters, capitalists or settlers, are usually
immediate; and the rewards of their enterprise must
be had in quick profits. Their economic interests are,
for the time, confined to present values." [2] With future values, the rightful inheritance of future genera-

three-quarters of the petroleum is left in the ground and rendered for ever irrecoverable—it is so that America, the richest
and the most wasteful and negligent of all lands, has set the
classic example of how an oilfield should not be developed"
(*ibid.*).

[1] *Proceedings of Joint Conservation Conference*, Senate Documents, vol. 10, No. 676. National Conservation Committee Report, p. 135.

[2] *The Foundations of National Prosperity*, edited by Professor
R. T. Ely, 1918, pp. 100-101. " That Smith's [Adam Smith's]
school teaches nothing else than the theory of values. . . . It is
. . . that science which teaches how riches, or exchangeable
values, are produced, distributed and consumed. This is un-
doubtedly not the science which teaches how the productive
powers are awakened and developed, and how they become
repressed and destroyed. M'Culloch calls it explicitly 'the science of values,' and recent English writers 'the science of exchange'" (*ibid.*, p. 74).

tions, the capitalist is naturally wholly unconcerned. In all that relates to the interests of future generations, "the making of profit" not only does not decide "whether labor has been wisely applied or material rightly used," but it actually inclines the mind of the director of enterprise to use labor for the destruction of the material necessary for future production.

We have next to notice the progressive deterioration in the quality of commodities brought about by the apotheosis of profit-making as the sole and sufficient method of organizing industry.   It used to be axiomatic that capitalist competition led to improvements in production.   What we now see, however, is that it leads no less certainly to deterioration in the products. When the sole measure of efficiency, and the only test of success, is the making of profit, the motto of the dictatorship of the capitalist is *non olet*.   Whatever yields profit is good; and the larger the profit the greater the assumed advantage to the community.   If the stimulus of gain has led to discoveries and inventions, by which the wealth of the nation has been largely increased, we see the same stimulus positively worsening the quality of the output.

THE WORSENING OF COMMODITIES

Adulteration, substitution, and all forms of short weight and false measure, tend to be regarded—to use

John Bright's classic phrase, as merely "methods of competition." [1] It was not until the middle of the nineteenth century that the public became aware of this form of competition; and it was the microscope that brought it to light. "Until the microscope was brought to bear upon the subject," we are told in the *First Report of the Select Committee on Adulteration of Food*, "no means existed whereby the great majority of adulterations could be discovered, and the parties producing them little dreamt that an instrument existed capable of bringing to light even these secret and guilty proceedings. Adulteration was then practiced in security, and with comparative immunity; now this feeling of security has been destroyed, and the adulterator knows that at any time he is liable to discovery." The leading medical witness demonstrated to the ordinary citizen the baneful effects of the much admired principle of free competition. "It may so happen, and it doubtless does sometimes occur, that the same person, in the course of a single day, receives into his stomach some eight or ten of the articles which I

---

[1] A contemporary of John Bright's explained this defense of adulteration. "If you could destroy the competition" of adulterated commodities, the Select Committee on Adulteration of Food was informed by the chairman of the Leamington Local Board of Health, "instead of working a benefit to the public, you would be working the greatest injury, because you would be creating a whole host of small monopolies in genuine articles, which would so increase the price of those articles that it would place them beyond the reach of one-third of the population" (*Second*) *Report of the Select Committee on Adulteration of Food*, August, 1855, No. 480, Q. 2535).

have enumerated. Thus, with the potted meats and fish, anchovies, red sauces, or cayenne taken at breakfast, he would consume more or less bole Armenian, Venetian red, red lead, or even bisulphuret of mercury or cinnabar. At dinner, with his curry or cayenne, he would run the chances of a second dose of lead or mercury; with the pickles, bottled fruits, or vegetables, he would be nearly sure to have copper administered to him; while if he partook of *bon-bons* at dessert, there is no telling what number of poisonous pigments he might consume. Again, at his tea, if mixed or green, he would certainly not escape without the administration of at least a little Prussian blue, and it might be much worse things. Lastly, if he was a snuff taker, he would be pretty sure to be putting up his nostrils, from time to time, small quantities of either some ferruginous earths, chromate of potash, chromate of lead, or red lead. If an invalid, his condition would be still worse; for then, in all probability, he would be deprived of much of the benefit of the skill of his physician, through the dilution and sophistication to which the remedies administered for his relief were subjected. This, I would remark, is no fanciful or exaggerated picture, but one based upon the legitimate conclusions derived from the analysis of different articles as sold to the consumer." [1] From

---

[1] *First Report from the Select Committee on Adulteration of Food, etc., with the Minutes of Evidence and Appendix*, July 27, 1855, No. 432, Q. 150.

this first inquiry in 1855 down to the present day, we
watch, in all capitalist countries, a rising tide of indignation against the complicated systems of adulteration
and substitution practiced by the profit-maker, with a
continually elaborated code of law for the purpose of
detection and restraint. If the microscope enabled the
public analyst to discover adulterations, the progress
of chemistry has enabled the profit-maker to use science to dodge the microscope. " The detection of adulteration," states a medical officer in 1915, " is becoming more and more difficult, and is due, in the first
place, to the astuteness of the vendors of the adulterated articles, and, in the second, to the more highly
scientific means now practiced. It has been pointed out
in previous reports that the vendors of milk ' tone ' it,
or, in plain English, adulterate it with separated milk;
but they take great care that they do not ' tone ' it
below the standard set up by the Board of Agriculture. The addition of separated milk to new milk has
become almost a fine art with some milk purveyors;
and, although they are known to receive large quantities of separated milk, which they do not sell, yet they
mix it so skillfully that it is impossible to bring them
within the four corners of the law." [1] " The chief
difficulty is with meat, the signs of disease in which
are difficult for the ordinary person to detect: they are

[1] Quoted in *Forty-second Annual Report of the Local Government Board*, 1915, Part III., p. lxvi.

frequently very easily removed; and as a last resort the sausage machine, spices, and a final attractive dressing as potted meat, pastes, sausages, or other delicacies, puts an effective disguise upon food which may be totally unfit for the purpose. The only place and time at which meat can be efficiently inspected is at the slaughter-house, just after slaughter, before any of the offal has been removed. . . . The circumstances at Grimsby are quite typical of provincial towns; ' there are fifty-four annually licensed slaughter-houses . . . scattered all over the town; and slaughtering may be in progress at all of them simultaneously at any hour of the day or night, Sunday included.' From the point of view of those whose care is for the wholesomeness of the meat supply, these facts constitute the justification for local public abattoirs and the abolition of private slaughter-houses." [1]　The demand, in short,

[1] *English Public Health Administration*, by B. G. Bannington, 1915, p. 160. "Here is a description of the private slaughter-houses given by a recent writer on the subject: ' often hemmed in by dwelling-houses on all sides, through ventilation in them is well-nigh impossible, the light sometimes can, but with difficulty, penetrate; the floor is often altogether unpaved, or so badly paved that the ground becomes sodden with blood and ordure; the walls are often made of wood that becomes saturated with filth; and the lairs are frequently insufficient to accommodate the animals.' To this might be added a large midden-stead into which, through a hole in the wall of the slaughter-room, the manure, offal and blood are swept, the floor level being specially arranged for this purpose. Around this sweltering mass of corruption the blue fly is present in myriads, and it is busy plying its deadly mission between the midden-stead, the slaughter-room, and the butcher's shop, as for the sake of convenience, they are all attached to each other " ("Municipal Inspection of Meat": a paper read by William W. Kelso,

is for the supersession of capitalist by municipal enterprise.

The elaborate regulations which all civilized countries have had to adopt for the detection and punishment of the profit-maker in his tricks and counter-tricks in worsening production, have been, in the main, restricted to foodstuffs and drugs. It has become recognized that this form of adulteration "means the gradual poisoning of a people, the lowering of the physique of a whole nation, the stunting of our growth, the rapid deterioration of our constitution; while morally it means a daily and constant fraud practiced by the seller on the buyer: a cheating which, begun with the smallest trifle, soon makes us so callous that it is applied with equally comfortable conscience to things of greater importance." [1]

The same process of worsening production is seen at work in all sorts and kinds of commodities and services: in the over-sizing of cotton cloth; in the manufacture of rickety furniture and of shoddy woolens for slop clothing; and in the " jerry-building " of the homes of all but the richest persons. Indeed, much of the odium which has been attached to

Chief Sanitary Inspector, Paisley, in Glasgow University at the Annual Congress of the British Institute of Public Health, July 27, 1896, p. 3).

[1] *Transactions of the National Association for the Promotion of Social Science,* 1870. (*Newcastle-on-Tyne Congress.*) *What Legislative Measures ought to be taken to prevent the Adulteration of Food, Drink, and Drugs?* by Phillips Bevan, p. 391.

machine production as compared with the more costly
handicraft is due to the ease with which the former
can be made to simulate soundness in commodities
which have lost the largest part of their value in use.
There is no reason why the machine-made chair or
window-frame, or the machine-made dress material or
boot, should be less durable, or even less artistically
designed, than the analogous hand-made commodity.
But division of labor and machine production, carried
on by capitalist profit-makers for immediate gain,
lends itself to, and in the end requires all kinds of
petty deceptions, many of which, like the " soaping together " of separate parts in slop clothing, are actually performed by hand.   Here again the capitalist is
aiming only at short-term success, and will often supply to the new markets which he has acquired by the
most expensive machinery for selling, commodities
which will be quickly " found out " as essentially un-
economical—occasionally even " not up to sample "—so
that all his compatriots in the business, and even his
own firm, will in a few years' time lose the market to
the traders of some other nation, who begin by supplying a better article, but, because they too are seeking
only profit, end by descending as low as the first.

This constant shifting of particular export trades
from nation to nation is one of the factors in the new
desire of the traders in each country for the use of
political influence to " secure " their markets.   Profit-

making enterprise, we are told by an American critic, "is in the hands of men who are single-minded in their competitive conduct of affairs. They neither are inclined, nor will business competition permit them, to neglect or overlook any expedient that may further their own advantage or hinder the advantage of their rivals."[1]

THE SUPPLY OF PERNICIOUS COMMODITIES AND SERVICES

To the capitalist profit-maker positive evil may be a good. The stimulus of profit-making works as potently in building up the vast industry of supplying futile or deleterious patent medicines, medicated wines, and proprietory cures for cancer, consumption, venereal disease, gout or rheumatism, not to mention abortifacients for the prevention of child-birth, as in that of feeding the hungry and clothing the naked. "The rate of profit in this business [quack remedies]," we are told, "remains high because many decent people do not choose to embark on it. . . . A man will buy only two or three boxes of pills, which can and do really cure him of an ailment, but he will continue to buy for years those remedies which never do him any good. This is quite a usual practice."[2] It is calculated that, in this business alone, over three million

[1] *The Theory of Business Enterprise*, by Thorstein Veblen, 1904, pp. 292-3.
[2] *The Laws of Supply and Demand*, G. B. Dibblee, 1912, p. 113.

pounds a year is extracted from the public in return for an expenditure of two millions on puffing advertisements—an expenditure which effectually silences the press with regard to this iniquitous trade. A mere fraction of the sum collected from the consumers— possibly £100,000—is cost of production, the remainder of the £3,000,000 being a " profit on price " which builds up great private fortunes.[1] The profitable industry of Tono Bungay is rivaled by that in which Mrs. Warren was engaged. In all the great capitals of the world millions of pounds are invested—some contributed by quite innocent rentiers—in dwelling-houses, tea shops, massage establishments, concert rooms, dancing halls, and other convenient covers for the profitable business of first decoying, and then interning girls and boys for the purpose of sexual vice. With this the economist must rank the promotion and organization of gambling in all its forms. Private

[1] *House of Commons Select Committee Report,* 1914, 414, pp. ix-x. Two remarkable publications by the British Medical Association on *Secret Remedies,* 1909 and 1912, give a series of analyses of all the principal proprietory remedies. This analysis reveals that whilst some of these patent medicines are positively injurious, the bulk of them are merely valueless, and are only distinguished by the enormous disproportion of the cost of production plus the government stamp, to the price paid by the consumer. The ingredients of a cough mixture at 2s. 9d. cost one-third of a penny; a shilling bottle of another remedy costs one-thirteenth of a farthing; an electric fluid advertised as a cure for cancer yielded nothing to analysis, whilst another mixture was water diluted with impure alcohol. Following on these revelations a Select Committee of the House of Commons was set up in 1914 which reported in favor of government analysis and control of all patent medicines—a measure not yet adopted, and not even within sight of adoption (1923).

gambling may or may not be a desirable pleasure. But
the deliberate stimulation and exploitation of the gambling instinct in men, women and young persons, for
the purposes of private gain—an industry employing
vast capitals—can hardly be accepted as a legitimate
utilization of the nation's capital, brain and labor. Another instance is the " service " of lending money at
hundreds per cent to minors and to temporarily dis-
tressed landlords or incompetent business men, or to
foolish clerks who have overspent their salaries.[1]

[1] The parliamentary secretary of the Local Government Board,
in introducing the Money Lending Bill in 1900, cited "two illus-
trations that came before the committee of the system against
which the Bill is directed. An unfortunate Irish landowner
named Finlay borrowed a sum of £300 from a money-lender, for
which he gave a promissory note for £456, the money being re-
payable in monthly installments. Mr. Finlay paid several installments regularly, and then for a subsequent installment the
check was sent a single day late. The check was returned and
the whole amount claimed. Default interest was charged, and
when Mr. Finlay came before the court he had been compelled
to pay, besides £114 in installments, a sum of £600—£714 in all—
for the loan of £300 from November 13, 1890, to February 20,
1892. . . . In the other case, an English firm named Adams borrowed £50 from Isaac Gordon in November, 1892, and signed
a promissory note for £200. Further advances were made of
£50 in February, 1893, of £20 in June and of £50 in November,
1893. Between November, 1892, and September, 1894, Mr. Adams
paid £461, and in October, 1894, Gordon claimed that £5PP was
still owing in respect to an advance of £220. . . . Gordon took
proceedings in the County Court at Birmingham on one promissory note" (Hansard, June 21, 1900, p. 681). The Bill had been
considered by a strong legal Committee who reported, that
"after carefully considering the evidence . . . your Committee
have unhesitatingly come to the conclusion that the system of
money-lending by professional money-lenders at high rates of
interest is productive of crime, bankruptcy, unfair advantage
over other creditors of the borrower, extortion from the borrower's family and friends, and other serious injuries to the
community" (ibid, pp. 682-3).

Finally, we have to note the fact that, as "civilization" advances, more and more of the land, machinery and labor of advanced industrial nations—more and more of the vaunted business ability that the all-powerful stimulus evokes—are diverted, first to the incitement, and then to the satisfaction of the world's "effective demand" for alcoholic drink of various grades of harmfulness—not to say for the production of, and the secret traffic in opium, cocaine and other deleterious drugs—which now account for so large a proportion of the fortunes on which families are founded and country houses maintained. Is it suggested that if the savings of each year were deliberately allocated to the extension and development of those branches of production which seemed most to need increasing—if these savings were administered by the democratically organized coöperative movement, by municipal enterprise, or through nationalized industries under the authority of Parliament, we should find anything like so large a proportion of the national dividend being used for these invidious, if not actually pernicious, purposes?

GAIN WITHOUT PRODUCTION

It is one of the ironic incidents in the enterprise of the private owner or organizer of the instruments of production that the accumulated capital of the nation

can be used for securing large profits on price without
producing any services or commodities whatsoever,
whether useful or deleterious. " The capitalist undertaker of old," we are told by the German exponent of
modern capitalism, " bore a technical impress. The
modern undertaker is quite colorless." He may decide to use the credit and capital which he owns or
controls in the manufacture of commodities or services, or he may find it more profitable to use it in
manufacturing " securities " which represent no assets
at all, but merely extravagant expenditure in advertising and booming what exists only on paper. "Henceforth, stocks and shares come into being, not because
of the needs of those who require money, and depend
on credit, but quite independently, as a form of capitalistic enterprise." [1]   The promotion of " wild-cat "
companies is in fact as perennial and as unfailing a
source of profit as the toilsome organization of useful
enterprises. " This class of fraud," solemnly explained
our greatest Lord Chief Justice in 1898, at the recep-
tion at the Law Courts of the Lord Mayor of London,
" is rampant in this community—fraud of a most dangerous kind, widespread in its operation—touching all
classes, involving great pecuniary loss to the community—loss largely borne by those who are least able
to bear it. And even, much more important than this,

[1] *The Jews and Modern Capitalism*, by Werner Sombart, 1913,
p. 101.

fraud which is working insidiously to undermine and corrupt that high sense of public morality which it ought to be the common object of all interested in the good of the community to maintain—fraud blunting the sharp edge of honor and besmirching honorable names." [1] " There was one case," continued the Lord Chief Justice, " in which a property was sold, or at least purported by the vendor to be sold—a property on the West Coast of Africa—for the sum of £48,000, when there was no property in existence at all. But an agent was sent out after this fictitious sale had been effected, whose report recorded the purchase of a property for the sum of £140 from a native chief, which the agent thought would nearly answer the description given of the fictitious property described in the prospectus. In another case a business, having been bought a few weeks before the formation of a company for a sum of £637, was sold to the public, who subscribed something like £76,650. These are the grosser cases. Another mode of fraud which is practiced—I am

----

[1] The buying of nobles, and other socially eminent persons who are without business training or capacity, as decoy-ducks to simple-minded investors is the converse to the public scandal of selling titles to wealthy parvenues who are without manners or morals. The 586 members of the House of Lords (including spiritual Lords) of 1900 shared among them " no fewer than 435 directorships or chairmanships of commercial concerns. On the list of peer directors of companies there are two bishops, nine dukes, eight marquises, fifty-three earls, nine viscounts, and eighty-one barons—all members of the House of Lords " (" Company Fraud and Parliamentary Inactivity," by J. G. Swift Macneill, Q.C., M.P., in the *Annual of the Co-operative Wholesale Societies, Ltd.*, 1900, p. 174).

speaking from my experience in Courts of Justice—is this: going to allotment on insufficient capital. The public did not subscribe as was hoped, and there was but a small amount of money from them. What, then, is to be done? An honest, independent, distinterested board of directors, who knew their business, would say that it was impossible to go to allotment upon such a subscription. But they are not their own masters; they are, in the cases which I have been supposing, creatures of the promoter, who pays them; they are not in a position to form an independent judgment. What is the result? The promoter gets hold of what money there is; and to carry on the company's miserable weak existence the directors issue debentures which are largely unregistered, and of which the creditors have no notice. They get an apparent amount of business carried on by the company; tradesmen and merchants deal with them; and, when the crash comes, down come the debenture-holders and sweep away their stock—every stick that belongs to the company—and the creditors are left without remedy."

A more subtle form of gainful enterprise is over-capitalization. "A concern which is honestly worth £100,000," we are told by the Lord Chief Justice, "and which upon that capital value might well pay a decent return for investment, becomes an imposition if inflated to satisfy the greed of the middleman and promoter to cover extravagant advertising charges, extravagant fees for expert reports, gifts in money or in shares to procure directors, aye, and even to procure the introduction of directors.   By these means it is offered to the public at an inflated price—at two or three times its actual value.   Need I say that in such cases loss and failure are certain, and the public are called upon to pay fees for the deception which has been practiced upon them? "   Even if it could be said that the boards of directors brought actual knowledge of business or strength of government to the concern it might at least mitigate the evil.   But it is notorious that in too many cases they bring neither one nor the other —neither knowledge nor strength—that they are chosen because it is supposed that their names or their titles might be attractive to the public.[1]   Indeed,

[1] *The Times,* November 10, 1898.   Lord Russell stated that the Official Receiver told him that from 1890 to 1897 " there had been lost to the community and gone into the pockets of the unworthy no less a sum than £28,159,482; made up of losses of creditors dealing with companies, £7,696,848; and of loss to the wretched contributories or shareholders, £20,462,633."   (These figures relate only to companies wound up compulsorily, and exclude cases of reduced capital.)   The loss of permanent situations by bankruptcies was pointed out by the Minority Report of the Poor Law Commission, 1909.   It was found by investigators into the causes which had brought men down to unemployment that bankruptcy or reconstruction of their employers' business held a high place.   " In 1899, a year of good trade, there were in England and Wales, 7,085 bankruptcies and deeds of arrangement with creditors.   In 1904, in the trough of the cyclical depression, the number was 8,631, or 22 per cent more (Twenty-fifth Annual Report by the Board of Trade on Bankruptcies, House of Commons, No. 254 of 1908).   If we assume that, on an average, only ten men lose their employment in each case, though the business does not always cease altogether, the statistics imply the loss of situations, through no fault of their

it has been discovered that business failures, with all
the depreciation and loss of capital that they cause, and
the tragedies of bankruptcy, unemployment,[1] and
family ruin that they involve, may be, for whole classes
of capitalists, from the firms who make a business of
supplying the perpetual crowd of venturous dupes who
start little retail shops, up to the promoters and fur-
nishers of mammoth hotels owned by companies destined to early "reconstruction," are as profitable as

own, by 70,000 men in a good year, and 86,000 men in a bad
year. And many small concerns fail and cease without formal
bankruptcy" (Minority Report, p. 572).

[1] We have omitted, because of its controversial aspect, the vast
subject of speculation on the stock exchanges and the produce
markets of the world. Some part of this speculation may be defended as an indirect, but we think cumbersome, way of equaliz-
ing prices. But legitimate speculation has in recent years been
submerged underneath an elaborate superstructure of commercial
gambling, not only in securities, but in essential food-stuffs and
raw materials; the dealings in "options" and "futures" in wheat,
cotton, etc.; the practices of "short-selling" and "rigging,"
"bolstering" and "hammering," "unloading" and "switching,"
in gambling on "specified margins," are all ways of getting rich
—often fabulously rich—without producing anything else but the
maximum amount of uncertainty in the earnings of all classes of
producers and in the prices paid by all classes of consumers.
"The chief attention of the business man," it is remarked by
Professor Veblen, "has shifted from the old-fashioned surveil-
lance and regulation of a given industrial process, with which his
livelihood was once bound up, to an alert redistribution of investments from less to more gainful ventures and to a strategic
control of the conjunctures of business through shrewd investments and coalitions with other business men" (*The Theory of
Business Enterprise*, Professor Veblen, pp. 24-5). Moreover,
this activity involves an actual increase of the risk and uncertainty of productive processes. "Broadly this class of business
men, in so far as they have no ulterior strategic ends to serve,
have an interest in making the disturbances of the system large
and frequent, since it is in the conjunctures of change that their
gain emerges" (*ibid.*, p. 34).

the laborious foundation of a flourishing new industry. We are never allowed to forget the " losses " incurred by the London County Council in organizing its own works department (to defend itself against a " ring " of contractors), and in taking up an enterprise in which private capitalism had failed miserably, namely, running a steamboat service on the Thames (to the health and enjoyment of many thousands of passengers) ; whereas nothing is heard, under " private enterprise," of the deliberate and continued abstraction from useful service of all the enormous amount of capital, ability, and labor that is being used, in the ways mentioned above, for socially unprofitable profit-making.

THE HYPERTROPHY OF SELLING AGENCIES

One of the most significant, and assuredly the least foreseen and least recognized, of the results of the profit-making impulse is the excessive development which it has brought about in the machinery of selling for selling's sake as distinguished from that of the production and legitimate distribution of commodities. The hypertrophy of mere trading and financing as sources of profit; the growth of tier after tier of parasitic middlemen; the expenditure, not only in one but in all highly organized capitalist states, of hundreds of millions of pounds a year in competitive and mostly mendacious advertising,[1] has already gone so far as to cause it to be said that it often costs more to sell an article, after it has been produced, than the manufacture of all its materials and all its component parts has required from end to end of the process, from plantation or mine to loading the finished product " free on rail " at the factory siding. It is scarcely an exaggeration to say that the dictatorship of the capitalist, under the stimulus of private profit, has brought us to this pass, that in the Britain of to-day a quarter —possibly even a half—of all the land, machinery, labor, and business ability of the nation is taken up merely in the profitable industry of putting into the hands of ourselves as consumers the commodities that we, as producers, have created.

It may be asked, Why not? It is not on the surface surprising that distribution should cost more than the more concentrated process of production. An obvious example is the water supply, in which the production

[1] G. B. Dibblee, in *The Laws of Supply and Demand* (p. 183), quotes Mr. Thomas Russell, president of the Incorporated Society of Advertisement Consultants, as estimating that a hundred millions sterling are spent annually on advertising in this country. "That is a very considerable figure, and it appears still larger when we note that the total engineering industries of this country, including shipbuilding and motor factories, had an output for 1909 in round figures of £150,000,000, of which £70,000,000 was due to the cost of material. Their net output of £80,000,000 is less than the advertising bill of the United Kingdom." The United States and Canada together would spend at least £250,000,000; Germany with Switzerland and industrial Austria about equal to this country; therefore we may reckon that the gross expenditure on advertising for Europe and North America is £550,000,000.

costs nothing and the distribution is enormously expensive. Any one who has witnessed the production of pins and steel pens by machinery or even of the cloth-bound sevenpenny book, will have no difficulty in believing that the conveyance of the finished article from the machine to the consumer is a far more lengthy and laborious task than its production from the raw material. Again as the product might as well not exist if its existence and uses are not brought to the knowledge of the consumer, advertisement has a legitimate function in national industry.

But the process of distribution developed by the profiteering system might more fitly be described as an elaborate system of interception and blackmail. The open road from the producer to the consumer becomes obstructed by a series of piratical turnpikes set up by persons who have neither made the road nor mended it, but predatorily squatted on a portion of it and set up a trade in wayleaves. Perhaps a more exact illustration would be a canal on which a number of unnecessary locks had been imposed, alternately raising and lowering the barges until they were finally delivered at the level at which they started and which they need never have left. And the profiteering advertisement gives information only as an incident of misrepresentation and seduction. For example, when the citizen has become possessed of an instrument, such as a sewing-machine or typewriter or motor car or what not, capable of doing him efficient service for ten years, extraordinary efforts are made by means of advertisement to induce him to purchase a new model every year; and changes are made—for better, for worse—in the instrument to persuade him that it has been improved, the change being as often as not either a matter of indifference or a positive disablement. It is the mass of "dead wood" or of actively cancerous tissue thus carried by the departments of distribution and publicity developed by the pursuit of profit that makes those departments so costly and so mischievous, and accounts for that hypertrophy of the selling part of the system of which we have given such unequivocal examples.

The cause of this hypertrophy is the perpetual anxiety of manufacturers and wholesale traders to obtain profit on an output which they are forced to increase continually without regard to demand. In the initial stages of capitalism, more particularly in the period when Great Britain had almost a monopoly of the machine process and the use of power, the output of commodities habitually failed to exhaust the effective demand of home and foreign markets. The world was still hungry for commodities. When Europe became satiated, eager merchants "had some pleasant years chasing the remaining hunger of the world and its attendant security of profit for themselves into odd corners of the East." So long as selling was a straightforward process, conducted by merchants whose main business was actually to transport commodities to places in which there was an effective demand for them at a higher price—literally to buy in the cheapest in order to sell in the dearest market—the axiom of the old economists that prices, in the long run, oscillated closely about the cost of production under the worst conditions worth facing at all, including the cost of transport, had some sort of meaning, the point being that any increased efficiency in the processes of manufacture, or any increased facility in the transport of commodities from the place of manufacture to the place of consumption, was followed by a decrease in the price to the consumer.

How "Over-production" Occurs

But with the extension of manufacturing enterprise on a large scale to all civilized countries this connection between increased efficiency and low price came to an end. Profit-making manufacturers and merchants, in their pursuit of increased profits through ever-increasing transactions, over-reached themselves. They produced in all the markets of the world temporary gluts of commodities, which they had either to retain at great cost or sell at a loss. "And here we come to the edge of the great problem of our gigantic industrial system," we are told by the acutest observer of this general over-development of the selling organization. "If we open the sluices of modern productive resources, developed under the factory system in the last seventy years, goods pour out at an amazingly cheap and ever cheaper rate, and the market is flooded beyond any possibility of commercial remuneration. The analogy is eminently appropriate without any laboring. No barriers of price could withstand the outflow; and the resulting inundation would mean the waste of the product and the probable destruction of the means of supply. Modern industry, therefore, besides the necessity of lowering the cost of production by a great expenditure of capital, has had to devote *an even greater aggregate capital* to a machinery for marketing the goods." "The productive power of modern industry is so tremendous," explains Mr. Dibblee, "that a comparatively small amount of capital laid down in some dozen suitable English, German, and American towns with a well-trained industrial population will be able to produce most kinds of goods capable of indefinite multiplication, sufficient for the whole world. But we are now talking of such large quantities, as without further mercantile organization could never be profitably absorbed." "It is not," he sums up, "production that is costly, but marketing. Since apparently *the greater parts of the rewards of industry go to those members of our commercial organization who are engaged in the adjusting duties of selling, buying, and selling again,* we have also to infer that there is some corresponding difficulty in these tasks which enables those engaged in them to gain their great rewards. It cannot be all chicanery and thievery." [1]

[1] *The Laws of Supply and Demand,* G. B. Dibblee, M.A., 1912 (pp. 43, 47, 52). One of the most interesting corollaries of this process of increasing price by diminishing cost of production, is the high salary earned by the expert seller of an article as compared with the expert producer of an article. "Take, for instance," remarks Mr. Dibblee, "the universally current expression of 'getting business'; that does not mean making shoes or marble clocks or cocoa, but finding customers for shoes, clocks, and cocoa. It shows the prevailing mental preoccupation of every one that a man who is reputed to be 'good at getting business' has *ipso facto* a ready market for his services in any line of commerce that he cares to undertake. The man who has that capacity and can plan to make production subservient to it has an easy road to fortune before him. It is the most valued talent in business, and one can be entirely without it who wishes to avoid failure" (*ibid.,* p. 180).

"What the economists have not so clearly brought out is the fact that on markets the middlemen owe their strength largely to their position at the center of exchange. They can take toll of the producer on the one side and of the consumer on the other; and (subject to extraneous competition or internal dissension) they have only to form a ring to manipulate both sides at once to their own advantage. What war again, with its tightening of organization and its urgent need for production, has shown up more clearly than the economists, is not merely the effect of bad or overpaid distribution on consumption and prices, but its reaction on production. Before the war the middleman was allowed to kill the goose that laid the eggs he dealt in; and nobody cared; food not produced at home could be imported. But war has raised the status of the goose. . . It should now be more evident where the money goes and why. Most fish markets are more or less close corporations; and the newcomer is not exactly received with open arms. Prices, in fact, are usually skied against him. But once he has achieved his footing, then it is to the interest of the older merchants to allow him to hang together with them as against the producer on the one side and the consumer on the other. In virtue of their position at the center of exchange, dealing on either hand with scattered and comparatively unorganized producers and retailers, the merchants are masters of the situation; and thus we find in nearly every port:

How Capitalism Increases Cost

This conclusion, as thus baldly stated, is not entirely convincing. The fact that an operation requires genuine ability does not guarantee its honesty. The burglar may be more skillful than the locksmith. But it is sound in its essential contention, which is, that the business of selling more products than the consumers really need, and of discovering fresh reserves of consumers, is a more difficult one than the business of production, and also an entirely different one. It thus becomes a separate branch: an industry in itself. And because it absorbs and retains a special class of profiteering ability, withdrawing it from production, and from simple direct distribution, it finally creates a class of middlemen who, from being at first indispensable to the manufacturers for the disposal of their surplus products, soon become indispensable for the disposal of all products by setting up a financial and commercial machinery of distribution which the producers and shopkeepers do not understand and cannot

" (1) That the salesmen and merchants are too many for the fish; and

" (2) That the accepted scale of charges and profits is keyed up, not according to distributive services rendered, but so that each one of the too many can draw a livelihood from his share of the fish passing through.

"If the small and inefficient merchant can charge the small amount of fish he handles with his livelihood, it is plain that, on the same scale of profit, the big and more efficient firm can draw a fortune from its larger quantity" (evidence given before the Committee on Trusts, 1916-17, "Rings among Fish Middlemen," Memo. by Stephen Reynolds, not published by the government).

work. Thus the middlemen become masters of the situation. They will not allow the producers and shopkeepers to compete and thus fix prices by the old higgling of the market. Their argument (until they are in a position to command) is, " That way lies ruin for us all." They fix prices themselves with an eye to their own profit, limited only by the point at which the consumers will go without rather than pay, and thus levying the highest toll on the most vital necessities. It is hardly half a century since the American economist, F. A. Walker, declared that the manufacturer as entrepreneur was supreme in the industrial situation. But the entrepreneur has lived to see his mastery pass to the financial middleman, who produces nothing, distributes nothing, but sells everything.

Thus arises the paradox, that the lower the cost of production of an article, including the cost of transport, the higher may be its price to the consumer, owing to the greater difficulty and expense of selling it. Or, in other words, increased competition means increased cost of selling, and this has to be added to the price charged to the consumer. The greater the competition, the higher becomes the retail price!

THE GROWTH OF MONOPOLY AND THE NEGATION OF INDIVIDUAL FREEDOM OF ENTERPRISE

The more astute or powerful of the organizers of the means of production in the United States of

America, Germany, and the United Kingdom were the
first to discover the fallacy of free competition, and
the disastrous results to the profession of profit-making
of "letting each man get rich in his own way." When
production had become "common form," and the
markets had been all explored, this competition in
cheapness, which was perpetually grinding, not merely
the faces of the poor but also the margin of the capitalist, naturally failed to commend itself to the up-to-
date business man as the short cut to riches. The
powerful profession of profit-makers, in spite of their
mutual distrust, could not fail to realize that combination would pay them better than the "cut-throat competition" which was always leading each of them to
magnify his own output, and to seek to dispose of it
by an indefinite lowering of price, or by raising the
cost of selling. We need not dwell on the recurrent
cycles of inflation and "over-production" that marked
the British and American business world from 1825 to
1887; or upon the genesis, during the past half-century, of the "gentlemen's agreements," rings, associations, cartels, trusts, consolidations, and amalgamations by which, in Germany and the United Kingdom
as in the United States, whole industries have passed
into the control of little groups of capitalist monopo-
lists. The most sensational examples of the inevitable
tendency to consolidate the interests of all profit-making capitalists within a single trade or industry are to

be found in the United States of America. Both American official reports and American fiction resound with the iniquitous doings, first of the American railway kings, and then of the great American trusts in oil, in meat, in copper, in steel and in innumerable other commodities. The growth of the German cartels, extolled by German economists as the last word of Teutonic capacity for organization, have been denounced by British business men who have been continually engaged, especially during the Great War, in imitating them! There is to-day, indeed, no hesitation among the captains of industry of any country in admitting the existence, and in justifying the working of these legalized conspiracies against free competition. "Prior to the formation of the Salt Union," stated its representative to the British Government Committee on Trusts, "there had been a period of very keen competition, with the result that most manufacturers were making little, if any, profit. Many were practically ruined." [1] "The cause of the formation of the association," stated the chairman of an important metal company to the same committee, "was the fact that this industry in Great Britain had been very unremunerative for many years, and had stood in danger of being crushed out of existence by foreign competition, and by too much competition among manufacturers at home; and it was realized that, if the industry

---

[1] *Statement by Salt Union Limited,* September 11, 1918.

was to be saved at all, the manufacturers would have
to come together and form an association. . . . By securing remunerative prices in the home market they
could make a successful bid against foreign competition in the export trade. They had a fund, a fighting
fund, for the special purpose of subsidizing members
who found it necessary to sell at less than an economic
price in order to cut out foreign competitors." [1]
" Trade organizations have in the past," testified the
chairman of the Sheet Makers Conference to the same
tribunal, " in many cases, put restrictions upon output;
they have realized that if more of an article is produced than can be sold, unprofitable prices must result.
The problem we have to solve, therefore, is how to
produce the maximum output and maintain profitable
prices, and in my opinion the only way is to adopt
the methods employed in the past with so much success by Germany. The trade organizations must become selling agencies. They then eliminate competition amongst themselves, in those markets where profitable prices can be obtained they get them, in other
markets where competition from other countries is
severe they must sell at the best prices obtainable—at
a loss if necessary—and so the maximum amount of
trade is done, and the burden of the unprofitable business is spread over the whole of the trade. In the past

[1] *Report of Committee on Trusts* (Ministry of Reconstruction), 1919 (Cd. 9236), p. 5.

it has paid Germany handsomely to export a large part
of her steel products at a loss. In the future it will
pay this country to do the same." " In the modern industrial and commercial world," summed up the Secretary of the Committee on Trusts in his learned
memorandum, " competition, which indeed never was
wholly ' free,' is becoming less free with each passing
year. In very many branches of trade and industry,
business concerns whose inter-competition is conven-
tionally supposed to maintain prices at a competitive
level have, in fact, working arrangements of one kind
or another which prevent competition. Again, in some
branches of trade, amalgamations of erstwhile rival
firms have taken place, with the result that in some
cases so large a proportion of the whole trade is in
the hands of one firm, or financially interwoven group
of firms, that an effective monopoly is obtained."[1]
Indeed, all the facts of modern industry prove conclusively that the competitive management of property
invested in industrial enterprise, and its management
in detail by individual owners, leads to hopeless inefficiency.[2]

[1] *Report of Committee on Trusts* (Ministry of Reconstruction), 1919 (Cd. 9236), p. 5.
[2] *Ibid.* The interesting reports made by committees of employers in each industry to the Board of Trade (1916-1918)
demonstrate the gross inefficiency in processes, mechanical plant
and organization within each of the staple trades. This is shown,
states the Departmental Committee on the Position of the Engineering Trades after the War, " by the very large number of
relatively small firms that exist—each with a separate organization, separate establishment charges, separate buying and selling

We need not ignore the industrial advantages of these successive concentrations, with their production of standardized articles on the most gigantic scale, and their progressive elimination of unnecessary costs. But in them, it is clear, the world loses a great deal of the individual initiative, the personal risk, and the freedom of enterprise with which the capitalist system

arrangements, and each producing a multiplicity of articles. Some of them seemed to take a special pride in the number of things they turn out; whilst few of them seemed to be willing to contemplate buying at a cheaper price a component part from a rival manufacturer, even if they were permitted to do so by that rival. A system of exclusiveness and aloofness marked the Engineering Trades before the war. Each manufacturer keeps his own secrets, and if he has any special method of manufacture, he, somewhat naturally, is desirous of retaining that process for himself rather than of adding it to the common manufacturing knowledge of the country. The result of many firms being employed upon producing a large number of articles in common use is the causing of confusion in the types of articles produced, so that no two manufacturers seem intentionally to produce precisely the same articles . . . there is consequently a very large amount of unnecessary stock of different patterns carried throughout the country and made at a higher cost than is necessary. Workmen are constantly diverted from the manufacture of one article to the manufacture of another; much time is thereby wasted, and the change over from machines entails a considerable amount of machinery standing idle when the special article for which that tool is required is not at the moment being produced. This is a wasteful and costly process, which limits output and therefore decreases possibility of profit and high wages, whilst the absence of much repetition work prevents a system of payment by piece being largely introduced." Indeed, the confessions and mutual accusations of employer and employed shows that, in the engineering industry at any rate, there was a persistence of "cacanny" alike among capitalist brain-workers and all grades of workmen—the employers accusing the British mechanic of deliberately restricting his output "below that which represents a reasonable day's work, and that this deliberate restriction does ultimately have a serious effect on his character and makes him physically incapable of producing a reasonable day's work through habit which this restriction en-

started, and by which it achieved its greatest triumphs. What is more serious is that the consumer loses that security against excess of price over cost; that guarantee of variety and quality; and even that assurance of abundance which free competition was assumed to afford him.

THE DRAWBACKS OF INDUSTRIAL CONCENTRATION

The progressive, though masked, usurpation of power by the capitalist becomes a dictatorship indeed, against which not the trade unionists alone, nor the socialists, but the whole world is in revolt. The first remedy to which American, Colonial, or British statesmen have turned has been the construction of complicated legal machinery, either for preventing trusts and combinations altogether, or for controlling their pernicious practices of restricting output and raising prices. But hitherto all attempts to police the capitalist monopoly have failed. In all capitalist countries rings, price associations, cartels, trusts, and amalgamations,

---

genders." On the other hand, the workers attribute this restricted output to the employer's practice of cutting piece-work rates, the workers' fear of unemployment, and the belief that the older or less experienced hands must not be handicapped by the superior productive powers of their fellow-workmen. (See also reports by the Departmental Committee on the Electrical Trades and Electric Power Supply, and " The Evidence before the Sub-Committee of the Advisory Committee of the Board of Trade on Commercial Intelligence for securing the Position after the War of Certain Branches of British Trade," Cd. 8275.) These committees of capitalists had one remedy only to suggest, namely combinations among British capitalists, supported by the political and military power of the British Empire.

some national and some international, extend from industry to industry, the aggregations of capital becoming ever larger, and their tentacles creeping upwards and downwards, monopolizing natural resources,[1] integrating manufacturing processes, controlling transport, and more and more dominating the markets of the world by their manipulation of prices and their regulation of output. "Competition is growing more and more feeble and ephemeral," summed up Professor Lester Ward: "combination is growing more and more powerful and permanent. . . . The coöperative tendencies of the rule of mind which destroy competition can only be overcome by that higher form of coöperation which is able to stay the lower form and set the forces of nature free once more."[2]

[1] The trusts are already reaching out to the control of what may be the next great source of mechanical power in industry, namely, hydro-electric energy. "An investigator has recently published convincing evidence that two great public utility organizations, the Stone and Webster and the General Electric groups, are systematically acquiring control of the undeveloped water power resources of the nation. . . . The rapidly increasing dependence of industrial and commercial activities upon hydroelectric energy will, at an early date, place magnificent values upon water-power sites. We know that tremendous speculative profits are assured by the acquisition and holding of such properties without the expenditure of a dollar of capital in their development. We know that the sources of industrial energy are so limited that the centralized and unregulated control of water power in the hands of a few private corporations would soon become the basis of one of the most powerful natural monopolies which may possibly be conceived" (*The Foundations of National Prosperity*, by R. T. Ely, etc., 1918, "Conservation and Economic Evolution," Ralph Hess, p. 159).

[2] *Annals of American Academy of Political and Social Science*, vol. iii., No. 4, January, 1893; *Psychologic Basis of Social Economics*, L. F. Ward, pp. 89-90.

The Apotheosis of Industrial Concentration

Now it is beyond dispute that the Great War has resulted alike in Britain and the United States, France, and above all in Germany, in accelerating, even more than is yet commonly realized, the process of amalgamation, horizontal and vertical, of the separate capitalist enterprises within each industry or group of industries, for the express purpose of putting an end to free competition for both the home and the foreign market. Nor can the economist complain of this. For one of the administrative discoveries under the stress and strain of the struggle for national existence was the failure, the almost sensational failure, of competitive profit-making to attain the maximum productivity, either in quality or in quantity. In one industry after another, in all the various countries, it was found that the more effective the competition among rival profit-makers the less efficient and economical was the process of production *regarded as an aggregate*. Hence, in spite of the overwhelming bias of capitalist governments against interference with competitive profit-making, government departments were driven to compel the capitalists to stop competing one with another, and to combine in gigantic organizations or associations, so as to utilize all their undertakings in the manner found to be most effective in maximizing the total supply. That is to say, when the governing class in each nation became really concerned for output, the " Court of Profit," with its unorganized juries of consumers, was set on one side; and the " Court of Public Audit," served by new classes of costing experts, uninterested in private profit, was given jurisdiction over capitalist industry. On the cessation of hostilities, governments bent on maintaining the reign of capitalism precipitately abandoned their new discovery of control. But whilst the " Court of Public Audit " was abolished, the " Court of Profit " was not reëstablished. As the economists have not failed to observe, " the habit of working together by standard methods for a common purpose has disclosed so many economies of business administration that, taken in conjunction with the obvious interest of price control in a period of grave financial and commercial insecurity, it has given a very important impetus to the pre-war tendency towards capitalist combinations. It is quite idle to suppose that the big combinations, especially in the metal and machinery trade, chemicals, and some branches of textiles and pottery, many trades supplementary to building, the railroad and shipping conferences, are likely to return to free competition." [1]

THE " FORCED ALTERNATIVE "

Thus the modern capitalist profit-makers, by eliminating the simple freedom of competition, have con-

[1] *Incentives in the New Industrial Order*, by J. A. Hobson, 1922, p. 16.

fronted the community with a forced alternative: either passively to submit to this capitalist dictatorship, now recognized and on the point of completion, or else establish without delay whatever social machinery may be required to enable the community to control the industries and services by which it lives. Either the trusts will own the nation or the nation must own the trusts. And this forced alternative is recognized even by clear-sighted Conservatives. "It would be very difficult to argue," writes Lord Hugh Cecil, "that it was more dangerous and mischievous to place all the means of production in the hands of the state itself than to have them monopolized by a number of private combinations. It is certainly true that the practical alternative before us is competition (at any rate among our own countrymen), or the control of the state, and that any effort to limit competition in the interests of any group of private persons, or anything less than the state, would be speedily judged to be intolerable." [1]

THE DIVORCE OF THE BRAIN-WORKERS FROM THE INSTRUMENTS OF PRODUCTION

The industrial revolution which took place in Britain during the last decades of the eighteenth, and the first decades of the nineteenth century, and, in the course of

[1] *Conservatism*, by Lord Hugh Cecil, 1912, p. 104.

that century, in the United States and the industrial-
ized parts of Europe, divorced, as we commonly say,
the manual workers from the ownership of the instruments of production. It was left to the growth of
joint-stock enterprise in the nineteenth century and
the merging of firms and companies in gigantic rings,
trusts and amalgamations, the capital resources of each
of which is counted in tens, and even in hundreds of
millions of pounds sterling, to carry to an extreme the
divorce of the brain-workers from the ownership of
the instruments of production, and to reduce them
also to the position of salaried employees. The past
three-quarters of a century in Great Britain, the past
half century in the United States, the last three or four
decades in Germany and France, have witnessed a
rapidly increasing separation of the great majority of
the organizers and managers of industry from the
ownership of the bulk of the material wealth embodied
in the land and buildings, the minerals, the machinery
and plant, and the means by which the product is
transported.

This has come about by gradual stages, as a mere
consequence of private ownership. In the management
and direction of industry, the operation of the law of
inheritance progressively interfered with the " selection
of the fittest." Sons reared in luxurious homes, and, to
say the least, not picked out for their profit-making
ability, succeeded to their fathers' businesses, which

gradually ceased to be marked by those qualities of initiative, discovery and enterprise which had served as a justification for the dictatorship of the capitalist. And the businesses did not, as may once have been the case in the eighteenth century, usually go into bankruptcy.

What has proved more and more practicable is the introduction of the hired brain-worker. Generation after generation saw an increasing number of enterprises directed by salaried administrators, on whom their otiose proprietors relied. The development of joint-stock enterprise in banking and in the larger forms of transport, and presently also in mining, manufacturing and trading on a considerable scale, revealed the unexpected fact that salaried management, under the supervision of boards of directors who were themselves more and more divorced from the dominant ownership of the concern, and were in fact only paid professionals in directorship, was quite capable of maintaining in existence, with reasonable dividends to the shareholders, large, varied and widely ramifying businesses. In some directions, such as banking, joint-stock enterprise under salaried management has, in nearly all countries, actually beaten the individual capitalist entrepreneur out of the field. In Britain the growth of mining royalties, the decline of the squirarchy, and the great development of house property in towns, have led to the substitution, for the active agricultural landowners, of a class of rent-receivers taking no more part in the management of real estate than the dividend-receivers in the management of industry, the two forming the *rentier* class now representing private property in France and Germany no less than in the United Kingdom and the United States. In this way ownership of the instruments of wealth production has accordingly now passed—in Britain to the extent of probably one-half of the whole wealth— to a steadily increasing class of functionless shareholders and rent-receivers, men, women and children, numbering possibly not more than 2 per cent of the population, who take no part in industry and mostly do not even know whence their incomes are derived. The aggregate income of these persons, who unashamedly " live by owning," amounts, apparently, to something like a fifth or a fourth of the entire product of the advanced industrial community.

THE GROWTH OF THE PROFESSIONAL CLASS

But the enormous growth of what John Stuart Mill called, three-quarters of a century ago, " the great social evil of an idle rich class," is not the most significant feature of the situation. Parallel with this development has been the growth, in all advanced industrial countries, of a still more numerous class of salaried brain-workers, of all grades, who, without the stimulus of profit-making, or any prospect of "making a fortune," beyond such modest provision for their old age and for their dependents as their saving may permit, are engaged, for the most part, all their lives, in different kinds of industrial and professional service.   A tiny percentage of this class receive large salaries and other emoluments, and may be classed with the capitalist directors of industry themselves, into whose ranks a certain number of them actually pass. But the vast majority of them serve all their lives long in such capacities as foremen, managers, accountants, scientific workers, and technicians of various kinds—even as designers, authors and inventors—for quite modest remuneration; while associated with them are an unnumbered host of clerks, salesmen, travelers and professional subordinates of every description.   Along with these must be ranked the rapidly increasing army of public officials of every kind, from the teachers of the publicly maintained schools and the various functionaries of the municipalities up to the highest administrators of the services that pass into State management.   Already before the war it could be said (without counting the army and navy) that more than a million persons in the United Kingdom were in the direct employment of either the central or local government, whilst cities like Glasgow or Manchester had as many as 20 per cent of all their households on the municipal pay roll.[1]

It is the upgrowth and the ubiquitous service of this *nouvelle couche sociale,* comprising now the vast majority of the active brain-workers in each country— honest, diligent, highly qualified for their work, and eminently successful in their function—which has reduced to absurdity the claim of the capitalist that only by the stimulus of profit-making and the ambition to " found a family " could efficient service of the community in the industrial realm be obtained. At the same time this " intellectual proletariat " discovers that the capitalist system has, for the great mass of brain-workers, practically no prizes. In many cases they find themselves pecuniarily worse off than the manual workers. They often earn less; their livelihood is sometimes more insecure; and they are in most cases subject to greater personal tyranny. More and more they are seeking a remedy in organization of the nature of trade unionism; and, like the manual workers, they are increasingly demanding for their professions the dignity and security of a public service. It is a significant fact that neither of them demands property as the remedy for their poverty. In spite of an agita-

---

[1] In such countries as Germany and France—as also in Australia and New Zealand—the proportion was even before the Great War considerably greater; although in the United States, owing to the continuance in capitalist hands of the railways, telegraphs and most of the tramway, gas and electricity services, it was smaller.

tion for what is called The Distributive State, which would abolish poverty by making every man an owner, the workers, whether by hand or brain, are practically unanimous in demanding honorable service as their means of livelihood.   It is this development of an honest, an efficient, and an instructed " salariat " which not only emphasizes the steadily narrowing sphere of the profit-making motive, but also, as we shall see, makes practicable an alternative system of industrial organization.

THE LOSS OF THE WHIP OF STARVATION

We now pass to the most potent, though hitherto the least recognized, factor in the progressive decay of capitalist civilization that has now set in.   In the political democracies of the twentieth century it has become more and more impossible to apply the whip of starvation.

Now it was by the whip of starvation brought to bear on the mass of manual workers, more than by the incentive of profit-making (which could, in practice, only become effective in a tiny minority of entrepreneurs), that the capitalist system achieved its initial almost automatic, success.   That is why the separation of the workers from the ownership of the instruments of production rather than the series of technological discoveries that transformed industrial

processes, is, to the scientific economist as well as to
the socialist, the essential feature of the Industrial
Revolution. The power with which the new capitalist
entrepreneur found himself endowed, of suddenly and
simultaneously throwing out of employment hundreds
and even thousands of operatives, having no alternative means of gaining a livelihood for themselves and
their families, was a new dictatorship, unknown in
medieval society, or even in the Britain or the North
American Colonies of the beginning of the eighteenth
century.[1] The alternate inflations and depressions of

[1] It is important to recollect that not only in medieval England but in the England of the seventeenth and early eighteenth
century, the majority of workers owned their instruments of
production and the product of their labor. The yeoman cultivator, the domestic manufacturer, the craftsman of the corporate
towns, with his journeyman and apprentice, might find himself
and his family on the verge of starvation through a bad harvest,
an epidemic or a great fire, a foreign war or the introduction
of a substitute trade or process. All these temporary disturbances to the accustomed livelihood seemed to him the Act of
God in no way altering his relation to the other members of the
community in which he lived. So long as the head of the little
industrial group owned the instruments of production and the
product of his labor and produced food or other commodities
for his own family and for his fellow-citizens, the fear of starvation through continuous unemployment, *and more particularly
unemployment deliberately caused by an economic superior,* was
practically non-existent. Moreover, what the peasant cultivator
or master craftsman lost by ill luck he more than made up by
the slow but continuous improvement in the processes of production characteristic of nascent capitalism. Thus we find during the first half of the eighteenth century a stationary population of turbulent workers, drinking heavily, eating largely of
meat, rollicking in the streets, betting and fighting at the fairs,
occasionally recruiting the much-admired profession of highway-
men, more often touring the country as professional vagrants,
and generally behaving so as to shock the pious justices into
forming Societies for the Reformation of Manners whilst giv-

each industry, the successive revolutions in industrial
processes and the ups and downs of foreign trade—
acting on populations newly herded together in the
expanding urban districts, where multiplication was
unrestricted—burnt into the minds of successive generations of the wage-earners that only by obedience to
the capitalist class could the propertyless man obtain
a livelihood for himself and his family. But, in England and Wales at least, there was, in the first half century of the machine-industry, one mitigation of this
new dictatorship. The able-bodied man to whom the
capitalist could or would not give employment at the
subsistence wage—a wage which might be, and indeed,
legally ought to have been, prescribed by the Justices
of the Peace—could, under the Elizabethan Poor Law,
demand to be set to work by the parish overseers, or
to have his scanty earnings made up from the Poor
Rate to the amount required to maintain himself and
his family, whilst full maintenance had to be provided
as a matter of course for all the non-able-bodied. We
have described elsewhere how the overseers of parish
after parish of England found themselves confronted
with hundreds, and sometimes thousands, of men,
women and children, rendered destitute by the capital-

ing endless opportunities of illicit gains to the notorious trading
justices who sprang up in urban districts. For a detailed description of the growth of destitution and pauperism coincidentally
with the Industrial Revolution see *English Local Government:
Statutory Authorities for Special Purposes,* by S. and B. Webb,
1922; and *The Parish and the County,* 1907, by the same.

ist refusal to continue them in employment, whilst new
Local Authorities were established under separate
statutes to establish workhouses, and to "set the poor
to work" in the vain hope of enabling them to produce their own maintenance. It is not surprising to
find that as the capitalist system spread, the total expenditure on poor relief, by which the stroke of the
whip of starvation was to some extent broken, increased by leaps and bounds. At the beginning of the
eighteenth century the total Poor Rate levied throughout England and Wales scarcely reached one million
pounds. During the ensuing three-quarters of a century it rose very slowly to a million and three-quarters.
Between 1776 and 1785 it suddenly bounded up by
25 per cent. At the beginning of the nineteenth century it had risen to over four million pounds, by 1813
to nearly seven millions, and by 1818 to nearly eight
millions. The peace of 1815, like the peace of 1918,
brought with it social conditions far worse than those
of the two decades of war. From the beginning of
1816, England was visited by an unexampled stagna-
tion of trade. "The poor," said Brand in the House
of Commons on March 28th, 1816, "in many cases
have abandoned their own residences. Whole parishes
have been deserted; and the crowd of paupers increasing in numbers as they go from parish to parish
spread wider and wider this awful desolation." [1]

[1] *Hansard*, vol. 33, p. 671; *The Life of Francis Place, 1771–
1854*, by Graham Wallas, 1898, p. 114.

The Episode of a Penal Poor Law

By 1832 it had become as clear as noonday to every enlightened person that the Elizabethan Poor Law was inconsistent with the capitalist system of industry. How could vast multitudes of men, women and children be made to toil and strain for twelve, fourteen and sixteen hours out of every twenty-four, frequently for less than a bare subsistence, and under wretched and unsanitary conditions, so long as there was always open to the able-bodied man and woman the alternative of being " set to work " on the parish stock, and to the non-able-bodied the indiscriminate idleness of the parish workhouse if not the freedom of outdoor relief; whilst for adventurous spirits there was the opportunity of being " passed " and repassed at the public expense from county to county in search of the parish of their settlement. We need not here repeat the oft-told tale of the wholesale pauperization of England under the reign of capitalism tempered by the carelessness of the parish officers, and the benevolent but misguided attempts of the Tory Justices to secure, by means of the allowance system, the national minimum of subsistence demanded and enforced by Tudor and Stuart legislation. Some way of escape from the horns of this dilemma had to be found. Hence the first great legislative achievement of the reformed Parliament of 1833, following on the enfranchisement of the new middle class of capitalist manufacturers, with their retinue of large and small traders and shopkeepers, was the famous Poor Law Amendment Act of 1834, expressly designed to make the condition of the pauper " less eligible " than that of the lowest grade of sweated worker. Every unemployed able-bodied man, whatever might be the cause of his unemployment, found himself confronted with the alternative, either of working at any wage and under any conditions offered by the capitalist profit-maker, or being incarcerated with scanty fare under a studiedly offensive penal discipline. The helpless rage of the British wage-earners against being thus handed over without appeal to the capitalist dictatorship found violent expression in the Chartist Movement; whilst the Trade Unions grew apace with their double purpose of meeting capitalism by combination with regard to the conditions of employment, and of insuring the members against unemployment.

But there was another force at work. The slow but persistent pressure of the wage-earners, through their Trade Unions and political organizations, for their political enfranchisement, led, in the United Kingdom, between 1867 and 1918, and in other countries during the same half century, to the adoption of manhood, and eventually even of adult suffrage, with political consequences of which we are only gradually becoming aware.

THE REPUDIATION OF THE PENAL POOR LAW

What has become apparent is that, just as a capitalist franchise proved incompatible with the Elizabethan Poor Law, a democratic franchise is incompatible with the penal Poor Law which replaced it. Right down to the twentieth century "enlightened public opinion," whether that of bishops or professors, of business men or civil servants, of devoted district visitors or able administrators of poor relief, still adhered to the "workhouse test" and to the principle of "less eligibility," as the only way of inducing men to prefer capitalist employment to Poor Law relief. Over and over again it was proved that, if the unemployed were given maintenance on a reasonably adequate scale, whether in the form of relief works or in that of the pauper dole, numbers of them would refuse to take work on the only terms offered by employers, and many of them would become unemployable through being maintained for long periods without work. Over and over again it was proved that any attempt to supplement, by outdoor relief or even by temporary sojourn in the workhouse, the sweated wage of the worst-paid workers, would increase the area of sweating and act as a subsidy to the most ruthless employers, who would immediately reduce wages by the amount of the supplement. But in spite of the continuous demonstration that disaster must follow any attempt

to combine the capitalist system with a return to the
Elizabethan conception of the right to " work or maintenance,'" each successive government, whether Liberal
or Conservative, found itself compelled to whittle away
the principle of " less eligibility."

It was expressly to stop this rot in the Poor Law
and its administration that the great Poor Law Commission of 1905-9 was set up, under the confident assumption that the Commission could not do otherwise
than recommend a return to the principles of 1834.
But here again the unseen forces of political democracy were at work; and not only the Minority but also
the Majority Report of the Commission (signed by
the representatives of the Local Government Board
and the Charity Organization Society) expressly repudiated the principle of " less eligibility," and denounced the workhouse test. But both reports coupled
this repudiation of the principle of " less eligibility " by
some provision for an adequate testing of the willingness of unemployed persons to accept employment
when it could be found for them, and to work in such
a manner that their services would be continuously required. This is not the place to discuss or criticize
these suggestions. What matters here is that public
opinion, expressed not only through the Labor Party,
but equally through the Liberal and Conservative Parties, flatly refused to supply the indispensable fulcrum
for the capitalist lever by making the acceptance of

capitalist employment virtually compulsory. All pro-
posals to register, test, and if necessary train, all destitute peresons who demanded to be maintained, and
could not under the law be denied, were repudiated.
In vain did the Guardians of the Poor point to able-
bodied paupers who lived cynically on the rates, demanding their discharge only to go out and earn
enough for a debauch before returning to the workhouse gate as destitute persons, and resuming their
residence there. The ratepayers clamored, the employers clamored, even the socialists (drawing a wide
moral) clamored against supporting men without
obliging them to produce what they were consuming;
but the mass of workers knew that capitalism had them
with their back to the wall, and that if the wall, stony
as it was, were demolished, there would be nothing
behind them but the abyss. During the years 1905-14
the machinery for giving subsistence to the able-bodied
unemployed, without tests, was enormously multiplied.
In 1920, capitalist industry, which had been virtually
superseded as a system during the war (otherwise the
war could not have been carried on), failed to keep the
machinery of production going, and completed the destruction of the semi-nationalized form which had just
saved the country. The consequence was that the
means of livelihood were withdrawn from millions of
British wage-earners through no fault of their own.
But they did not starve; nor did they go into the work-

house. In spite of every desire to curtail public expenditure, and of an openly avowed intention of forcing down wages, the British Government found itself driven, in 1921-3, to provide maintenance for every unemployed worker, either by way of Outdoor Relief on what would at any previous period have been deemed an extravagant scale, or else by weekly doles direct from the Exchequer at rates actually exceeding the wages offered by employers in some counties to the agricultural laborers. Something like a hundred million pounds a year were thus distributed among a couple of million families for years together. This completed the demonstration of the incompatibility of capitalism with democracy. It is impossible not to see in this the warding off, as regards the one-fifth of the entire population who would otherwise have felt the lash of the capitalist whip of starvation.

The inevitable conclusion is that, if political democracy endures, the adoption of the policy of " work or maintenance " at the public expense is henceforth certain. And this work or maintenance, afforded by central or local governments to all who claim to be unemployed, will, we predict, necessarily have to be free from penalization and from the stigma of pauperism. Even the tests of destitution, with which the Poor Law experts of 1834-1900 thought it essential to load the public succor, are doomed. For to any such clogging of the provision for those to whom, through no fault of their own, the capitalist system fails to find employment at adequate wages, the great majority of the electorate strongly objects. So long as the community notoriously allows a minority to be " above the law of nature and morality that if a man does not work neither shall he eat " : that is to say, so long as a definitely parasitic class of idle rich is permitted its habit of " conspicuous waste," the representatives of the wage-earning class are justified (and will be upheld in their contention at the polls) in objecting to the law being applied to the most innocent of the non-workers, namely, those prevented from working by the capitalists' failure to perform the task they have undertaken.

It will be said here, and said very cogently, that democracy may say what it pleases and vote how it pleases, but that any system under which a large section of the population can obtain maintenance for themselves and their families without being required to accept work at such jobs and at such wages as are actually obtainable then and there, must lead to national bankruptcy; and that if it be an objection to the capitalist system that it enables thousands of the population to live in idleness, a system which enables millions to live in idleness is in that respect an intolerable aggravation of the evil. This is true: and it was this consideration that carried the Poor Law of 1834 into effect in spite of a popular hatred of it which, though not at first enfranchised, would nevertheless have wrecked the measure, had the Chartists been able to convince the nation that there existed a then practicable alternative. Nowadays the alternative is quite familiar, and was so even before the war had given a stupendous proof of the possibility, and even of the necessity, of superseding capitalism and substituting public organization and control of industry. Even those who in defiance of the experience of the war believe that this is a dream, cannot deny that the people are dreaming it, and no longer fear that pulling the linchpin out of the capitalist apple-cart is pulling the linchpin out of human society.

Besides, the capitalist, to whom access to virtually compulsory labor is a matter of life or death, is forced to resist any legal compulsion to labor. His whole object is to make himself and his family and descendants independent of their own exertions by establishing them in genteel idleness. When he is brought to the point and asked bluntly whether he is in favor of making labor legally compulsory, he cannot say yes, because the next question from his workmen will be, " Is it to be compulsory on your sons as on ours? " That is checkmate: if there is to be compulsion to work by the withdrawal of supplies or by any other method [1]

---

[1] It is needless to remind the reader that in previous periods of depression accompanied by a penal Poor Law, large masses of vagrants have sprung up and have been dealt with not by the withdrawal of supplies but by penal imprisonment. One of the apparently good results of universal maintenance for unemployed persons under the Insurance Act and the lax administration of

it must clearly apply to all able-bodied idle persons without distinction of birth or education; for equality before the law is, under political democracy, an essential condition of its enforcement.

Take as an example of this the extraordinary obedience of the vehicular traffic of London to the rule of the policeman. An observer standing at Piccadilly Circus during the busiest hours will fail to discover a single instance in which the authority of the constable directing the traffic is defied, evaded or even resented. But imagine what would occur if the law privileged all persons of title, or all payers of supertax, or all owners of motor cars to defy the rule of the road, and go right or left at what speed they chose. At once, at least in the Britain of the twentieth century, every other person would claim for himself a like privilege; and the enforcement of any rule would become impracticable. During the war of 1914-18, nothing was more remarkable than the very near approach to universality with which the nation accepted the various disciplinary measures that were deemed

outdoor relief has been the relative absence of vagrancy: few unemployed men being willing to take "to the road" at the cost of giving up unemployment benefit. It is not so universally recognized that any withdrawal of this maintenance would mean an immediate recrudescence of vagrancy with a demand for the prosecution and punishment of any person found wandering "without the means of subsistence." But this would be countered by an immediate agitation for the prosecution and imprisonment of all persons without the *method of subsistence, i.e.,* without a recognized way of earning their livelihood by producing commodities or services for other people to consume.

necessary. But imagine how impossible it would have been to have enforced, on the four-fifths of the population who are wage-earners, either military service or food-rationing, if the " gentlemen and ladies " of property had been exempted from the law.

Thus capitalism finds itself in a cleft stick. Democracy has taken its whip out of its hand; and the only other instrument of compulsion available to make men work for it would be laid across its own back, and would thereby withdraw from it the peculiar privilege and sole reason for existence of the whole *rentier* class, of living above the first law of nature and morality, that " if a man will not work, neither shall he eat."

Its sole consolation is a rather dangerous one socially. When the unemployed were left to starve, or to face the misery and contempt deliberately inflicted on them by the 1834 Poor Law, the peril of insurrection was so obvious that it had to be staved off in times of special stoppages of trade, as in the case of the cotton famine caused by the civil war in America, by huge public subscriptions and relief funds. This peril did not prevent lock-outs and wholesale discharges of " hands " in slack times; for these are essential features of capitalist commerce; but it had some effect in making the employers think twice before they produced desperate situations without absolute commercial necessity. To-day, owing to the almost universal provision of a weekly income for every unemployed man, the employers can indulge their caprices and make speculative changes without the risk of finding their factories besieged and their houses burnt by starving rioters. Even the completely discredited "Allowance System," by which the insufficient earnings of men actually in employment are brought up to something like subsistence level, was, in 1922, beginning to be reintroduced in England; either in the form of alternate weeks of wage-earning and unemployment benefit, or, in cases of continuously employed agricultural laborers and sweated women-workers, by weekly supplement from the Poor Rate.

Now is it really necessary to repeat once again the old, old truth—always being reinforced by events—that distribution without equivalent production means ruin through exhaustion? The pernicious anæmia of a slowly but continuously increasing area of maintenance without work may well prove a more deadly disease than the destruction of capital and the capitalists by a bloody revolution. There can be no permanence in a situation in which we abandon production to capitalism, and yet give the workers the political power to enforce demands on the national income which capitalism has neither the ability nor the incentive to supply. It is a situation in which those before cry Forward and those behind cry Back.

This incompatibility of political democracy either with a landed aristocracy or a trading autocracy was

prophetically perceived by no less stalwart a squire than
Oliver Cromwell, to whom, significantly enough, the
Liberal Ministry of 1894 erected a statue paid for by
its wealthiest member.   Poring over those illuminating
debates in the Council of War at Reading in 1647, we
watch Cromwell and Ireton spending day after day in
trying to persuade their officers and men that " That
which is most radicall and fundamentall, and which if
you take away there is noe man hath any land, any
goods, [or] any civill interest, that is this: that those
that chuse the Representors for the making of Lawes
by which this State and Kingedome are to bee govern'd, are the persons who, taken together, doe com-
prehend the locall interest of this Kingedome; that is,
the persons in whome all land lies, and those in Corporations in whome all trading lies. . . . If wee shall
goe to take away this fundamentall parte of the civill
constitution, wee shall plainly goe to take away all
property and interest that any man hath, either in land
by inheritance, or in estate by possession, or any thinge
else." [1]   It was useless for the protagonist of the contemporary radicals, Colonel Rainborow, to assert, " I
doe nott finde anythinge in the law of God, that a Lord
shall chuse twenty Burgesses, and a Gentleman butt
two, or a poore man shall chuse none.   I finde noe

[1] *The Clarke Papers: Selections from the Papers of William
Clarke,* edited by C. H. Firth, for the Camden Society, 1891, vol.
i., pp. 302-3.   And see *English Democratic Ideas in the Seventeenth Century,* by G. P. Gooch, pp. 202-226.

such thinge in the law of nature, nor in the law of
nations. But I doe finde, that all Englishmen must bee
subject to English lawes, and I doe verily believe, that
there is noe man butt will say, that the foundation of
all law lies in the people. . . . Therefore I doe [think]
and am still of the same opinion; that every man born
in England cannot, ought nott, neither by the law of
God nor the law of nature, to bee exempted from the
choice of those who are to make lawes, for him to live
under, and for him, for ought I know, to loose his life
under." [1]   Again and again Cromwell and Ireton re-
iterate that if "one man hath an equall right with
another to the chusing of him that shall governe him
—by the same right of nature, hee hath an equal right
in any goods hee sees: meate, drinke, cloathes to take
and use them for his sustenance. . . . If the Master
and servant shall bee equall Electors, then clearlie those
that have noe interest in the Kingedome will make itt
their interest to chuse those that have noe interest. *Itt
may happen, that the majority may, by law, nott in a
confusion, destroy propertie; there may bee a law
enacted, that there shall bee an equality of goods and
estate."* [2]   (The italics are ours.)   At last Colonel
Rainborow ironically retorts: " Sir, I see that itt is impossible to have liberty butt all propertie must be taken

---

[1] *The Clarke Papers: Selections from the Papers of William
Clarke,* edited by C. H. Firth, for the Camden Society, 1891, vol.
i., pp. 304-5.
[2] *Ibid.,* p. 307.

away.   If itt be laid downe for a rule, and if you say
itt, itt must bee soe." [1]

The Economic Case Against Capitalism

We can now sum up the strictly economic case
against the continuance of profit-making capitalism as
the sole, or even as the main method of owning and
directing the instruments of wealth production, before
we proceed to the last count in the indictment, the relation of the process of profit-making to wars between
nations and classes.

In the first three chapters we described the adverse
results on the mass of the people of the dictatorship
of the capitalist.   In spite of an enormous increase in
the aggregate production of commodities and services,
due to the application of physical science under the
potent stimulus of the desire for profit, capitalism has
been everywhere accompanied by persistent insecurity
and chronic penury among the wage-earners, together
with a widespread morass of destitution.   And although the rise and growth of a new wealthy class may
not, in itself, have increased either the insecurity and
penury of the mass of the people, or widened the sur-
rounding destitution, the contrast adds a further grievance, whilst the encouragement of parasitic idleness,
the sterilization of intellect and the decay of manners

[1] *Ibid.*, vol. i, pp. 304-5, 315.

among the newly enriched, are social evils paralleled
only by the servility, the envy, and the corruption of
ideals manifest in the slum population. Besides, the
inequality in personal fortune, which is admittedly inherent in capitalism, produces, as we have seen, an evil
of its own.   In all communities where division of
labor has developed from the domestic division of the
primitive farmhouse to generally organized industrialism, the great majority of the workers are necessarily
wholly occupied in performing technical operations
which transform materials into products or rendering
services which are part of organized systems of service.
They must therefore be at the orders of the relatively
few persons whose business it is to buy materials, to
sell products, and to organize services. This natural
necessity places a power in the hands of these few persons which, unless it is controlled in the general interest, as it is in the public services, can and does become
a tyranny compared to which the worst political tyrannies are negligible. When it is wielded by the irresponsible private owners of the sources of production, or by their agents, the disparity of effective freedom—"the opportunity for continuous initiative "—
is such as to amount to the practical subjection of the
mass of the people. This subjection disguises itself as
subordination; but in genuine social ordination the
director is no more free to give orders as he pleases
than his subordinates are to work as they please. The

capitalistic owner and director is entirely insubordinate, whilst his employees are helplessly subordinate; and thus the necessary and beneficent subordination becomes a mischievous and oppressive subjection. How tremendous is the new power over other people, which capitalism thus gives to the propertied class, is seen, for instance, in the peremptory closing-down of works or mines, as a means of starving the workers of whole districts into submission, and in the irresponsible determination, by this class, through the decisions of the directors whom it supplies for the industry of the nation, of the physical environment in which millions of their fellow-citizens shall pass their lives: in the devastation of the pleasant countryside, the pollution of the streams and the atmosphere, the creation in the slums of the new urban centers of all the conditions of disease and premature death, which have everywhere accompanied the mining, metallurgical and manufacturing enterprises of capitalism in the pursuit of private gain. And the social result is made no better—is even made worse—by the fact that alike in Britain and France, the United States and Australia, the propertied class has known how to escape from the adverse environment which—without, as is only fair to say, being fully conscious of what it was doing—it has created for its wage slaves. Equally unexpected, either by the economist or the moralist advocates of the unrestricted enterprise of the owners of the instruments of produc-

tion a century ago, and perhaps until our own generation seldom consciously sought by the capitalists themselves, is the typical phenomenon of twentieth century
democracy, in which private wealth, concentrated as to
direction into relatively few hands, is seen very largely
to control, by its dominion over the newspaper press,
the mental environment of the whole population; and
by its power in this and various other ways, even to
nullify universal suffrage, and dangerously to influence,
in the interests of private gain, the executive government and the legislation of every advanced industrial
community.

The False Judgments of the " Court of Profit "

In the present chapter we have brought into view
some of the developments of capitalism itself, which
seem to us, from the outset, to undermine the economic
arguments by which the dictatorship of the capitalist
was supported. The experience of the world, whether
in countries of advanced industrialism or in those newly
opened to capitalist enterprise, has revealed that the
tremendous stimulus of profit-making is undiscriminat-
ing. If the capitalist finds that he can enrich himself
more quickly by a reckless consumption of the irreplaceable mineral resources of the community, by the most
wasteful utilization of its forests and by the exhaustion
of its agricultural fertility—ruinous as this may be to

the permanent economic interests of the community—
there is nothing to prevent, or even to dissuade, such
a use of the dictatorship involved in the private ownership of the means of production. In the "Court of
Profit," by which Charles Booth thought it so satis-
factory that all capitalist enterprise was necessarily
tested, the widespread stripping of the world's forests
for the advantage of a single generation; the waste of
its accessible resources in coal, oil and gas; the exhaustion of its virgin soils, by which, as we now see,
the United States and Britain have shown themselves
as improvident as the barbarians—were approved and
applauded as " good business " even from an actuarial
standpoint. In like manner, the insidious worsening of
commodities, so long as the consumer could still be in-
duced to buy, might be, and was frequently proved to
be, productive of a greater percentage of profit, and
often of a greater aggregate income to the individual
profit-maker, during the whole continuance of his business, than the supply of articles of a better quality.
Not even the most optimistic defender of capitalist
enterprise has been able to allege that the verdict of the
" Court of Profit " coincides with that of any judge
of soundness of material, artistic excellence, perfect
adaptation, durability, or, taking all things into account,
even cheapness to the purchaser. Much more serious,
however, has been the discovery, to which the economists and moralists were for a whole generation aston-

ishingly blind, that, when capitalism brings its enterprises for judgment into the " Court of Profit," that court can pay no heed to evidence that the profit-making enterprise is entirely divorced from any public service. Within the wide scope given by the penal code all pursuits are alike valid, all saleable commodities and services equally permissible. The destruction of commodities, whether fish or a bumper crop of cotton, in order to maintain prices is no less a " productive " enterprise than adulteration or substitution in order to lessen cost. The smuggling of opium into China or whisky into the United States, like the manufacture of cocaine in a foreign factory, or the organization of gambling in another country—both being crimes in that in which the capitalist happens to reside—are as legitimate sources of gain as the growing of wheat. The whole industrial organization may, as we have seen, be distorted by the fact that greater profits can be made by the financing, and even by the selling of commodities than by their production, in such a way as to lead to the creation of an altogether disproportionate amount of social machinery of middlemen for the mere dealing in commodities, to which both producers and distributors find themselves paying unnecessary or excessive tribute. In the " Court of Profit " the mere fact that any profit is actually made, without demonstrated transgression of the criminal law, is accepted as conclusive proof of equivalent social service.

THE FUNDAMENTAL FALLACY OF LAISSEZ FAIRE

Why does the "Court of Profit" give, in all these cases, what the world now sees to be false judgments? It is because the basic assumption, which commended capitalism to the moral conscience of the nineteenth century, is now seen to be without foundation. The world no longer believes that, if every person without exception, capitalist or wage-earner, rigidly pursues his own pecuniary gain—and even pursues it with knowledge and wisdom—this will necessarily coincide with the greatest aggregate pecuniary advantage of the community as a whole. We know now that personal and corporate interests not infrequently conflict, even within the sphere of pecuniary gain : the individual may make profit by all sorts of manipulation without rendering service; whole classes may live by mere tribute, whether the fruit of commercial monopoly, or of more reputable rents, royalties and dividends; finally, the entire population of one generation may, as we have seen, with the full approval of capitalist ethics, for its own gain waste the substance of all future generations. There is no such "invisible hand," as Adam Smith romantically suggested, always guiding the dictatorship of the capitalist, even without his being aware of it, so that it promotes the economic welfare of the community.

Let us avoid any appearance of overstating the case.

Though the existence of profit is, as we have seen, no proof that social service has been rendered, it is instructive to note within what limitations the judgment of the " Court of Profit " may afford a test of business enterprise. As between one profit-maker and another, for instance, the judgment of the court may have a certain validity. It may be a test of relative efficiency in human labor and of the ability exercised in its direction and in the purchase and sale of materials with a view to the greatest commercial profit. But it does not, and by its very nature cannot, decide between rival enterprises one of which aims at profit and the other at something else.

COMPARISON OF COST

There can be no comparison in that court between a patent medicine manufacturer, making profits by the million pounds, and a public hospital making none. It can never be an effective tribunal as between enterprises having different ends. What is needed for this purpose is not a skilled and impartial assessment of profits, which one of the parties (say a private electric lighting company) is aiming at maximizing whilst the other (say a municipal electric supply) must minimize on pain of being convicted of malversation, but that objective measurement and publicity which is the method of science. And here we see that the very divorce, not only of the manual workers but also of the great mass of brain-workers, from the ownership of the instruments of production, to which the further development of capitalism has led—the rise in advanced industrial communities of whole classes of independent experts, from physicists and engineers, chemists and biologists, to analysts and surveyors, accountants and auditors— is creating an alternative court of appeal. During the Great War, the costing expert determined, not which process yielded the greatest profit, but which produced the goods at the least cost. And here we see how it is that the supersession of the test of relative profit-making by that of relative cost and relative production implies a stride onward in knowledge as well as in organization. This enables us to understand why it is that, in the Britain of to-day, it is the Labor Party with its socialistic aims, and not the Liberal Party or the Conservative Party, as adherents of the capitalist system, which deliberately puts in its program the advancement of science.

THE PROBLEM OF AUTHORITY

For without the application of the scientific method to social organization the crucial problem of democracy, the problem of authority—how we can obviate the arbitrary exercise of one man's will over another— cannot be solved. Hitherto it has always seemed, to the wage-earner, that the vital question in social organization is who should give orders and who should obey them—whether the government of industry shall be " from above " or " from below." Experience shows that both these ways of exercising authority have their special drawbacks.   In the ensuing years of ever-increasing socialization this controversy will become largely meaningless.   Strange as this may seem to-day, we venture on the prediction that, from the standpoint of personal authority, it will matter far less than at present exactly how the executive command is apportioned.   In industry no less than in political administration, the combination of measurement with publicity is to-day already undermining personal autocracy.   The deliberate intensification of this *searchlight of published knowledge* we regard as the corner-stone of successful democracy.   The need for final decision will remain, not merely in emergencies but also as to policy; and it is of high importance to impose heavy responsibility for a decision, according to the nature of the case, on the right people.   How, for this purpose, those democratic institutions that have been for a whole century encroaching on capitalism? whether central or local government, consumers' coöperation or vocational organization? can be further developed and coördinated, so as to provide for the exercise of ultimate authority in industry, we have described in another book.[1]   What

[1] *A Constitution for the Socialist Commonwealth of Great Britain,* by S. and B. Webb, 1920.

we want here to point out is that, owing to the advance of science, a great deal of the old autocracy, once deemed to be indispensable in government departments and capitalist industry alike, is ceasing to be necessary to efficiency, and will, accordingly, as democracy becomes more genuinely accepted, gradually be dispensed with.

The stream of decisions or orders by which the wheels of industry are kept going will cease to be the exercise of one man's arbitrary will over other men's actions. The independent professional, whether costing auditor or efficiency engineer, medical man or educational adviser, will report according to his knowledge; but he will give no orders and exercise no authority. His function is exhausted when his report is made. His personality will find expression, and his freedom will be exercised without limitation, in the process of discovery and measurement, and in the fearless representation of whatever he finds without regard either to the *amour propre* of the management or to the rebellious instincts of any grade of employees. Those who are " in authority," whether directors, managers or foremen, trade union executives or shop stewards, will give their instructions with these expert reports before them. They will exercise their authority under the searchlight of published knowledge; a searchlight which will encourage, if not compel them to feel their responsibility, not merely to sections, but to the whole community. A steadily increasing sphere will, except in matters of emergency, be found for consultation among all grades and sections concerned, out of which will emerge judgments and decisions arrived at, very largely, by common consent. This common consent will be reached by the cogency of accurately ascertained and authoritatively reported facts, driven home by the silent persuasiveness of the public opinion of those concerned. Under any genuine democracy it is, in the last resort, public opinion that decides; and the more effectively public opinion is educated and the more weight is given to the findings of science, the greater will be the success of any administration. In place of the jealous secrecy in which thousands of rival engineering establishments at present enshroud their operations, and of the bureaucratic concealment which to-day marks alike the Post Office and the government dockyards, we foresee the administration of each national industry and service, no longer concerned for magnifying the private gains of particular capitalist groups, or enhancing the net revenue of the Exchequer, but merely for increasing the efficiency of the service to the public, in the glare of a whole series of searchlights, impinging at different angles upon what is essentially the same problem, namely, how to obtain for the community as a whole the greatest possible efficiency in relation to the efforts and sacrifices involved. To quote the words with which we end our *Constitution for the Socialist*

Commonwealth of Great Britain, " What we visualize is a community so variously organized, and so highly differentiated in function as to be not only invigorated by a sense of personal freedom, but also constantly swept by the fresh air of experiment, observation and verification. We want to get rid of the ' stuffiness ' of private interests which now infects our institutions; and to usher in a reign of ' Measurement and Publicity.' " [1]

[1] *A Constitution for the Socialist Commonwealth of Great Britain,* by S. and B. Webb, 1920, pp. 355-6.

CHAPTER VI

THE CAPITALIST SYSTEM AS A CAUSE OF WAR

In the foregoing analysis of the morbid growths and insidious diseases to which capitalist enterprise is now seen to be increasingly prone—growths and diseases which lead to the inference that profit-making capitalism, with all its initial advantages, has now ceased to be, on balance, profitable to the community—we have dealt exclusively with its effect upon the aggregate production of material wealth. There still remains to be considered an even graver indictment of the capitalist organization of industry, and of the profit-making motive on which it depends, namely, that this system has, in modern times, become increasingly the cause of disastrous wars between nations. Indeed, if we limit our survey to the most advanced industrial communities, during the past half century, it is not too much to say that the struggle for pecuniary profit among rival groups of capitalist entrepreneurs may be recognized as having been the most potent cause, though usually an underlying and partially hidden cause, of recent international conflicts, including, in particular, the culminating calamity of 1914-18. What with these national wars, and, as we shall describe, what with

194

the equally injurious class war that capitalism so obviously provokes, it becomes a matter for the gravest apprehension whether, if it is not immediately controlled in the public interest, and progressively replaced by some better organization of industry, with some other incentive than profit-making, the reign of capitalism is not destined to destroy civilization itself.

War Between Nations

Let us first consider the close connection between the highly developed capitalist system, with its increasing hypertrophy of trading and financing and concentration of production in little monopolist groups controlling a colossal output, and the growth, during the last few decades, of a predatory imperialism among the great powers, at last issuing in the Great War of 1914-18.

So long as British manufacturers and merchants had a " natural monopoly " of the raw materials and markets of the world, they were indifferent to the growth of the British Empire, and regarded even territories colonized by British people as almost useless encumbrances involving expense to the British taxpayer. But with increasing competition among themselves, and with the entry into the world-markets of the manufacturers and merchants of the United States and of the German Empire, not to mention the " rising sun " of Japan, the political faith and economic doctrine of the British profit-makers gradually changed to suit their altered circumstances. To insure the continued profitable disposal of the huge output of commodities characteristic of these world-wide trusts and amalgamations, there was needed, not only command of the sources of supply of raw materials, but also a position of dominance in foreign markets, free from hostile protective tariffs, and able to forestall, by protective tariffs of their own, the potential competition of producers in other nations who were outside the combination. Hence, from being convinced free traders, " little Englanders " and anti-militarists, the British capitalists of the last decades of the nineteenth century became increasingly distrustful of their old creed, and more and more sympathetic to Protection, and to the extension of the *Pax Britannica* to all corners of the earth by a powerful navy and a costly expeditionary army. John Bright, the cotton manufacturer of the middle of the nineteenth century—a period when British cotton goods held the markets at home and abroad—was the protagonist of cosmopolitan pacifism. Joseph Chamberlain, his great successor in the leadership of the Radicals, fresh from establishing in the United Kingdom what was practically a monopoly in the manufacture of screws, became convinced by the end of the century that " the Empire . . . is commerce. . . . It was created by commerce, it is founded on commerce,

and it could not exist a day without commerce. . . .
For these reasons, among others, I would never lose
the hold which we now have over our great Indian
dependency—by far the greatest and most valuable of
all the customers we have or ever shall have in this
country. For the same reasons I approve of the continued occupation of Egypt; and for the same reasons
I have urged upon this government, and upon previous
governments, the necessity for using every legitimate
opportunity to extend our influence and control in that
great African continent which is now being opened up
to civilization and to commerce; and, lastly, it is for
the same reasons that I hold that our navy should be
strengthened until its supremacy is so assured that we
cannot be shaken in any of the possessions which we
hold or *may hold hereafter.* . . . If the little Englanders had their way," he added with scorn, " not only
would they refrain from taking the legitimate opportunities which offer for extending the empire and for
securing for us new markets, but I doubt whether they
would even take the pains which are necessary to pre-
serve the great heritage which has come down to us
from our ancestors." [1]

The powerful but crude imperialism of the leading
British statesmen was reënforced by the more polished
but more pointed utterance of the leading British pro-

[1] *Foreign and Colonial Speeches,* by the Rt. Hon. Joseph
Chamberlain, M.P., 1897, pp. 101-102, 131-133.

consul. " You cannot have prosperity without power,"
stated Lord Milner in an address to the Manchester
Conservative Club in 1906, " you, of all peoples, dependent for your very life, not on the products of
these islands alone, but on a world-wide enterprise and
commerce. This country must remain a great Power
or she will become a poor country; and those who in
seeking, as they are most right to seek, social improvement, are tempted to neglect national strength, are
simply building their houses upon the sand. ' These
ought ye to have done, and not to leave the other
undone.' But greatness is relative. Physical limitations alone forbid that these islands by themselves
should retain the same relative importance among the
vast empires of the modern world which they held in
the days of smaller states—before the growth of Russia
and the United States, *before united Germany made
those giant strides in prosperity and commerce which
have been the direct result of the development of military and naval strength.*" [1]   (The italics are ours.)

The Trail of the Financier

After the manufacturers and merchants of Great
Britain came the financiers. When capital has accumulated in large fortunes, when the rate of interest

[1] *The Nation and the Empire: Being a Collection of Speeches
and Addresses,* by Lord Milner, G.C.B., 1913, p. 140.

at home begins to fall, the discovery is made that there are many uncivilized races, and some races whose ancient and pacific civilization does not permit them to defend themselves, who can be more easily exploited than fellow citizens. " The maximum amount of harm," we are told by Lord Cromer, " is probably done when an Oriental ruler is for the first time brought in contact with the European system of credit. He then finds that he can obtain large sums of money with the utmost apparent facility. His personal wishes can thus be easily gratified. He is dazzled by the ingenious and often fallacious schemes for developing his country which European adventurers will not fail to lay before him in the most attractive light. He is too wanting in foresight to appreciate the nature of the future difficulties which he is creating for himself. The temptation to avail himself to the full of the benefits which a reckless use of credit seems to offer to him, are too strong to be resisted. He will rush into the gulf which lies open before him, and inflict an injury on his country from which not only his contemporaries but future generations will suffer." [1] Hence the export of capital becomes even more attractive to the profit-making capitalist than its utilization in the extension of manufacturing facilities at home, or the provision of the most urgently needed public services. If trade follows the flag, the flag has to reciprocate by follow-

[1] *Modern Egypt*, by the Earl of Cromer, vol. i., 1908, pp. 58-9.

ing the money-lender in order that it may protect him from his disappointed and enraged creditors. Moreover, there are always the traders and financiers of the other great capitalist Powers, equally anxious to exploit the barbaric man. " There is commonly a handsome margin of profit in doing business with these pecuniarily unregenerate populations," explains the American critic in the *Theory of Business Enterprise,* "particularly when the traffic is adequately backed with force. But, also commonly, these peoples do not enter willingly into lasting business relations with civilized mankind. It is therefore necessary, for the purposes of trade and culture, that they be firmly held up to such civilized rules of conduct as will make trade easy and lucrative. To this end armament is indispensable." [1] But in the portioning out of the trade per-

---

[1] *The Theory of Business Enterprise,* by Thorstein Veblen, 1904. One of the most glaring instances of capitalist influence, on Imperial policy has been afforded by the story of the forcing of opium on China. It is in relation to the " Opium War " of 1839-42 that Dr. Arnold wrote to a friend, " Ordinary wars of conquest are to me far less wicked than to go to war in order to maintain smuggling, and that smuggling consisting in the introduction of a demoralizing drug which the Government of China wishes to keep out, and which we, for the lucre of gain, want to introduce by force." The policy of the Chinese government was expressed by the Emperor's manifesto in 1847. "I cannot," he said, " prevent the introduction of the flaming poison; keen-seeking and corrupt men will, for profit and sensuality, defeat my wishes; but nothing will induce me to derive a revenue from the vice and misery of my people" (*Parliamentary Report, China,* 1847, p. 297). The capitalist traders, shipowners and bankers interested in the China trade had their way, and " the drug sold as a poison in England, specially prepared to minister to the weakness of the Chinese, has been poured into their country at the rate of a ton per hour for the twelve hours of every

quisites that fall to the proselytizers any business community is in danger of being over-reached by alien civilizing powers.   No recourse but force is finally available in disputes of this kind, in which the aim of the disputants is to take advantage of one another as far as they can.   A warlike front is therefore necessary; and armaments and warlike demonstrations have come to be a part of the regular apparatus of business, so far as business is concerned with the world market." [1]   "A state of commerce," we are told by a leading German industrialist, "has always been in a certain sense a state of war—a peaceful state of war, if one may use the word, which served peaceful ends as long as peace lasted, but which always lent itself to warlike designs, whether there was a war or not." [2]

THE UNASHAMEDNESS OF IMPERIAL CAPITALISM

Thus we see in all capitalist countries the armament makers, often using subsidized newspapers, pressing

day for some sixty years; whilst, to add to the wrong, the great Dependency which reaps the immediate revenue is united and emphatic in its condemnation of the particular vice from which it draws its profit" (*The Imperial Drug Trade*, by Joshua Rowntree, 1905, p. 268).   The Chinese revolution in 1911 at last brought the system to an end, the British and Indian governments agreeing to stop the export of opium.   Unfortunately, with the anarchy into which China has fallen, the capitalists have again begun this lucrative traffic.

[1] *The Theory of Business Enterprise*, Thorstein Veblen, 1904, pp. 295-6.

[2] *The Iron Circle: The Future of German Industrial Exports*, pp. 46-7.

close behind the peaceful penetration of the capitalist profit-maker. There is, however, one refreshing feature about the manufacturers of and the traders in the weapons for human slaughter. Their vocabulary contains no cant about humanitarianism; they are not even guilty of using the cloak of patriotism. The manufacturers of warships and torpedoes, of rifles and cannon, of shrapnel and high explosives, are completely indifferent as to the character and nationality of their customers. The same amalgamation will have factories in different countries, and on its board there will sit the industrial magnates of rival nationalities. They " do business " impartially with the government of their own country or with the governments of allies or potential enemies. What suits them is not a League of Nations, nor even a " balance of power," but an unstable equilibrium, producing scares in one country after another, so as to lead to the maximum world expenditure on armaments. And who can blame them? Did not Adam Smith teach us that " the natural effort of every individual to better his own condition, when suffered to exert itself with freedom and security, is so powerful a principle that it is, alone and without assistance . . . capable of carrying on a society to wealth and prosperity." What Adam Smith did not foresee was that this same self-regarding principle, abnormally intensified and distorted by the international scramble for neutral markets, is equally potent in dragging society into the most devastating of wars, and likewise, as may now be added, into the most disastrous of all recorded international settlements after war, exactly because this Treaty of Versailles was based on the fundamental principle of commercial capitalism: "the profits to the victors."

How Wars Occur

The moral is that it is not possible to confine the effect of great armaments, patrolling the globe for the protection of profit-making enterprises, to the intimidation of half-civilized debtors, the enforcement of commercial contracts, and the defense of factories and commercial garrisons. If what is called "peaceful penetration" results in the presence of a foreign warship in a national harbor, a fort will inevitably be built capable of sinking that warship lest it should be made the instrument not only of commerce but of dynastic ambition and conquest. Such a fort will lead to another and more heavily armed ship; and such another ship to another fort with guns of longer range. The same strain is set up by a military expedition. Its purpose may be to enforce the payment of interest on a foreign loan in an imperfectly commercialized country, or to clear desert trade routes or what not. But the inevitable result is the appearance of another military expedition to keep the first one within bounds, as, for example, when Kitchener, having secured the interest on the Egyptian loan and " smashed the Mahdi," found himself suddenly under suspicious observation by a French expedition under Major Marchand, with the immediate result that relations between France and England became dangerously strained, and France, getting the worst of it for the moment, set to work to reenforce her military position in Africa very markedly.

If capitalism could control the diplomatic and military situations it thus inevitably creates, Cobden's dream of a universal peace founded on foreign trade might not have been wholly illusory. But it is impotent in the face of the national passions, the international jealousies and terrors, the romantic pugnacities roused by its attempts to use national armaments as a trade police. It cannot even pursue these attempts with pacific integrity : the establishment of an effective police in its completeness means nothing short of conquest and annexation; and these mean war, which, though colossally profitable to certain trades for the moment, involves an appalling destruction of capital and thrusts a ramrod into the financial machinery on which the whole business of foreign trade, and consequently of much domestic trade, depends. Hence, though the great world war of 1914-18 was an inevitable incident in the pursuit of outlandish markets by capitalism, the capitalists, when the fatal hour struck, recoiled from the war as sincerely as the conscientious objectors

themselves, and had to be swept into it by entirely uncommercial romantically patriotic considerations and
passions, knowing that the destruction of capital, the
dislocation of commerce, the diversion of labor on a
gigantic scale from production to slaughter and ruin
would overwhelm all their best-laid schemes. Thus it
is equally true to say that the City made the war and
that the City was against the war. In short, in diplomacy and war, the profiteer hegemony is omnipotent
for evil and impotent for good. It can bind; but the
sword has to loose.

Britain's Share

We may now summarize the relation between the
dictatorship of the capitalist and the nearly continuous
warfare that followed the inauguration of world peace
by the London Exhibition of 1851, and culminated in
the monstrous catastrophe of 1914-18. It was the
British capitalist who, fortified in his faith by the early
political economists, first made of the pursuit of pecuniary gain what we may not unfairly call a national
religion. It was British publicists who provided a
rational basis for the callousness of the big manufacturer in his slaughter of children and his maiming of
young people of his own race through the early factory
system. It was a priest of the Established Church of
England, the Rev. Thomas Robert Malthus, who de-

clared that death by starvation for those who were
thrown out of work and deprived of wages by the ups
and downs of foreign trade was not only a "natural
law" but also "God's law" for adjusting the population to the means of subsistence.   It was, in fact, British commercialism that prepared the moral conscience
of mankind for the German theory of world power.
Bismarck and Treitschke were the spiritual descendants
of Ricardo and Nassau Senior.   In the last quarter of
the nineteenth century we watch the conscious extension of this idealization of profit-making to national
statecraft, by the deliberate molding of a nation's foreign policy to the purpose of augmenting the profits
of its capitalist entrepreneurs; profits to be derived, be
it noted, not from a common international progress in
production and exchange, but, specifically, from the
pecuniary loss of the business men of other nations.[1]

[1] The rapid extension of "Imperialism" is definitely ascribed,
by a competent French authority, to the "prodigious expansion"
of European industrialism.   "The application of steam to industrial purposes," he says, "put into the hands of the capitalist
an incomparable force, greatly multiplying his power, but at the
same time as the several nations saw their productive power
and their riches increase, they found their wants also increase,
so as to become imperious.   They presently became aware of
the narrowness of the boundaries within which they had formerly
lived at their ease; and they demanded for their industries ever
more raw materials and ever larger markets.   To secure materials, to conquer markets became vital to nations and governments.   Economic rivalries took the place of merely political
quarrels; and behind the Colonial ambitions there lurked always
the imperative requirements of the struggle for existence.   It
becomes daily more clear that the strength of any State is to be
measured entirely by its financial, industrial and commercial resources.   The trader has become the monarch of all the world.

This identification of motive in the individual capitalist and the state was openly proclaimed in the policy of the German Empire after 1871. " The one sound basis of a great Power which differentiates it essentially from the petty state," declared Bismarck, " is political egoism and not romanticism; and it is unworthy of a great state to fight for what is not connected with its interest." [1] The moral philosopher may question

In olden times the Christian nations appeared to savage peoples in the guise of the Conquistador, clad in armor, marching with the sword in one hand and the Gospels in the other. To-day it is the trader who is the pioneer of civilization. He goes ahead. He precedes the missionary and the soldier. Our utilitarian time finds glory only in the number, the intrepidity and the wealth of its traffickers. The proudest apostle of Divine Right, the Emperor William II., did not shrink, on one memorable occasion, from the following utterances, which would have remarkably surprised his 'unforgettable ancestors' whose memory he is so fond of recalling. 'Let all my traders out there realize,' he said, 'that the German Michael has firmly placed upon that land his buckler bearing the German Eagle, in order to assure them of his protection.' All these territorial rivalries, all these diplomatic quarrels are at bottom nothing but the competitive struggles of rival traders. It was a trading company, the Chartered (South African Company), which came near, a few years ago, setting South Africa in flames. It was another trading company, the Niger, that, more recently, sowed dissension between France and England. It was, they say, a trading syndicate that brought about the Cuban war. Finally, the iniquitous war, which, at the moment of writing, is being waged between a handful of stout fighters and the whole force of the British Empire was caused— if London phariseeism will permit to say—by the insatiable appetites of a band of financiers and business men. Cecil Rhodes himself has acknowledged as much with cynical frankness. 'This war,' he says, 'is a just one, because it has for object the protection of the British flag, *which represents to-day the great commercial impulse in the world.*' Everywhere the trader is in front; the governments are his obedient servants; and soldiers go to their deaths to fill his coffers " (*La Conquête de l'Afrique*, par Jean Darcy, 1900, pp. 3-5).

[1] *Bismarck*, by C. Grant Robertson, 1918, p. 66. Bismarck may have been the first statesman of the nineteenth century who was frank in his avowal of egoism as the principle of national policy.

whether the German version of the struggle for existence was not less ignoble, though possibly more dramatically dangerous, than its English forerunner. "My country, right or wrong," is, we think, a less debased guide to feeling, thought and action than "my own pecuniary interests, right or wrong." And those who delight in argument from analogy may find justification for this preference in the relative psychology of the dog and the cat. The dog, we are told by the experts of the new psychology, derives its descent from an animal that hunts its prey in packs and possesses in a highly-developed form the herd instinct; whilst the cat is related to the tiger that kills for himself alone, and is therefore incapable of the impulsive self-devotion which the dog habitually shows as the companion of the man. The followers of Adam Smith, like the tiger and the cat, left no place for self-devotion and self-sacrifice, seeing that it was the pecuniary interest of the individual, or at best of the individual and his family, that was to be alone considered. The passionate patriotism of the German race, however distorted by dog-like devotion to the Fatherland, had, at any rate, the quality of the voluntary self-sacrifice of the individual to the power and wealth of the community to which he belonged. But this distinction between British and German morality does not complete the picture. The German people had some justification in feeling that equity as well as national self-interest was embodied in an aggressive policy. When the German manufacturers, traders and financiers came into the world market they discovered, or thought they discovered, that at least a quarter of the trade of the world had followed the flag of the British Empire,[1] while the United States of America and the Russian Empire dominated more than half of the remaining territories and populations. Was it surprising that the German government, and even the German people, sincerely believing with Joseph Chamberlain and Lord Milner that profitable commerce with the undeveloped countries was dependent on national prestige, on "spheres of influence" and fiscal protection, felt that they were hemmed in, and deprived of their legitimate share of the profits to be derived from the exploitation of the labor and resources of other races? The Court, the General Staff, the civil administration, the bulk of the university professoriate, and the leading industrial and financial magnates, be-

[1] The universality among other nations of this feeling of resentment against the British Empire had been admitted two years before the war, by a leading British imperialist, successively member of the Coalition and of the Unionist governments of 1920-23. "Meanwhile a great change was taking place in Europe. By 1870 the long struggle for German and Italian unity had been achieved and an internal equilibrium established in Europe which has now lasted for over a generation. A great expansion of European industry followed, and with it a desire for territorial expansion and naval power. But in its efforts to extend its territories or acquire a colonial empire, every power found itself confronted with the British government, either in actual political possession, or jealously watchful of the vested interests of a commerce spread all over the world, and acutely alive to the menace implied in the steady closing of every market controlled by protectionist rivals" (*Union and Strength*, by L. S. Amery, M.P., 1918, p. 91).

came obsessed with the desire to augment the German
export trade at the expense of the export trades of other
nations. If peaceful means did not prevail, rapidly
and completely, why should not they call in aid the
power created by the Prussian capacity for military
organization? Had not the British government, time
after time, called in the British fleet to round off and
complete the encircling British Empire? It was in this
way, we suggest, that the apotheosis of individual
profit-making led inevitably to the Great War.

The Class War

But incalculably grave as is the indictment of capitalism as constituting the underlying cause of war between nations, there is a further count. War between
nations, even on so great a scale as that of 1914-18,
is only episodic. More continuous and universal, and
therefore probably more potent in its effects on society,
is the class war which the capitalist organization of
industry, with profit-making motive, has gradually
created in every advanced industrial community. We
now see the Owenite Trade Unionism of 1834, the
Chartist Movement of 1837-48, the uprising of the
workmen of Paris and Lyons, Dresden and Vienna in
1848, the violent outburst of the Paris Commune in
the defeated France of 1871, together with the abortive
Russian revolution of 1905, as only the precursors of

a movement of revolt by the manual workers, which to-day extends to nearly every nation, and, in countries of advanced industrialism, falls not far short of being co-extensive with the whole wage-earning class. For as the capitalist system became dominant, in one country after another, the wage-earners had burnt into them, generation after generation, the doom of perpetual penury, varied only by recurrent destitution through unemployment, to which, as a class, they were condemned. They necessarily realized far more keenly than any other section of the community the deprivation of personal freedom that their poverty involved: a deprivation all the more galling in contrast with the almost boundless increase of freedom which the new wealth production brought to those who reaped the swelling profits. It was the manual workers, and their children, on whom fell the ever-increasing toll of industrial accidents and industrial diseases, which the capitalist system brought in its train. It was their class that suffered the physical and moral degeneration, the sickness and premature old age that resulted, in Britain, from the unrestrained profit-making of the early-Victorian mines and factories, and from the unregulated urbanization of the countryside. The long spells of recurrent unemployment characteristic of the modern machine industry, in the United States as well as in Britain, which seemed to an enlightened capitalist like " the orderly beating of a heart, causing the blood

to circulate—each throb a cycle," [1] may possibly mean
to the successful brain-working entrepreneurs a greater
stimulus to exertion and inventiveness: to millions of
manual workers they mean involuntary idleness with
insufficient food, and with this food obtained, if obtained at all, through the demoralizing process of doles.
Not until the later part of the nineteenth century were
the bulk of the manual workers sufficiently educated to
organize an industrial and political revolt against a
system of conducting industry, against which their
leaders had never ceased to protest.   The twentieth century found the feeling of a class war—of an irreconcil-

[1] It is a curious example of vocational bias that so enlightened
and public-spirited a man as the late Charles Booth, could deliberately summarize the effect of recurrent and long-con-
tinued spells of unemployment on the life and labor of the
people in the following way:

"Looked at from near by, these cycles of depression have a
distinctly harmful and even a cruel aspect; but from a more
distant point of view, 'afar from the sphere of our sorrow' they
seem less malignant.   They might then, perhaps, with a little
effort of the imagination, be considered as the olderly beating
of a heart causing the blood to circulate—each throb a cycle.   Even
in the range of our lives, within easy grasp of human experience,
whether or not men suffer from these alternations depends on the
unit of time on which economic life is based.   Those who live from
day to day, or from week to week, and even those who live from
year to year, may be pinched when trade contracts—some of them
must be.   There are some victims, but those who are able and
willing to provide in times of prosperity for the lean years which
seem inevitably to follow, do not suffer at all; and, if the alternations of good and bad times be not too sudden or too great, the
community gains not only by the strengthening of character under
stress, but also by a direct effect on enterprise.   *As to character,
the effect, especially on wage-earners, is very similar to that exercised on a population by the recurrence of winter as compared
to the enervation of continual summer.*"   (The italics are ours.)
(*Life and Labor of the People in London,* by Charles Booth,
1903, Second Series; *Industry,* vol. 5, pp. 73-4.)

able cleavage of interest between the "two nations"
in each land—rapidly spreading to nearly every section
of the wage-earners, in practically all countries in which
the capitalist system had become dominant.

Let us note that this secular struggle of the wage-
earners against the capitalists has varied, in its capacity
for sheer destructiveness and its incapacity for social
reorganization, according to whether the dictatorship
of the capitalist has or has not been tempered by the
reign of democracy within the state. Under the ruthless and corrupt autocracy of Russia with its complete
exclusion of the town workers and peasants from participation in the government, the leaders of the "Bolshevik" or "majority" section of the socialist movement, when suddenly loaded with the responsibilities of
government by the revolution of 1917, were forced to
abandon all pretense of democracy, and establish "the
dictatorship of the proletariat," which was certainly a
dictatorship, but under it, as before, the proletariat was
dictated to, and the government prisons were as full,
and its rifles as active, as those of the Tsardom, in
spite of the sincerity of its aim at the common good.
In the well-ordered and highly-civilized autocracy of
Germany, tempered as this was by a wide suffrage and
a semblance of parliamentary institutions, the rapidly
growing socialist party accepted the Marxist shibboleth
of dictatorship of the proletariat without deciding
whether it meant, as Marx meant by it, a phase of

martial law ruthlessly administered by the victorious revolutionists, or government by the representatives of the people as a whole, the majority of whom would necessarily belong to the manual working wage-earning class. This ambiguity of phrase, and failure to think out clearly the steps to be taken, involved a disastrous division of opinion in the workers' ranks, and sterilized, for the first years after 1918, the otherwise powerfully organized Labor and Socialist movement. In Britain, Sweden, Denmark and Belgium, and in Anglo-Saxon Australasia, countries in which political democracy had been firmly established, the first decades of the twentieth century saw the rise in the legislatures of a definite Labor and Socialist Party, demanding, and to some slight extent beginning, the reconstruction of society, on a socialist basis, but avowedly limiting itself, as a democratic party, to constitutional methods of political democracy. Even in these countries, the Labor and Socialist parties bear the stigmata, in the diseases of democratic infantilism from which they suffer, of the environment in which they have been bred.

We must therefore solemnly warn our capitalists and governments that if they are well advised they will no longer dare to say " After us the deluge," or to depend on its fury spending itself in Russia and sparing us to muddle through without unpleasant incidents. The working classes have been even more deeply commercialized in some respects than the capitalists, because the capitalists become rich enough to follow the ancient Greek precept, " First gain an independent income, and then practice virtue." The late Andrew Carnegie practiced virtue, even civic virtue, on a stupendous scale when he had built up a colossal fortune on the ruthless exploitation of Pittsburgh. But the working classes never reach the turning-point: they are struggling desperately for an income all the time, and cannot exercise the Carnegian virtues, or acquire the moral amenities which go with them. Thus the capitalist, ever thinking of the rate of profit instead of social service, is reflected in the workman thinking only of wages and hours; selling himself to the highest bidder; and, on business principles, assuming that he should give as little as possible, for as short a time as possible, in return for as much as possible. This sort of sale is in its essence prostitution; and it cannot be imposed on generation after generation of workers without finally disabling them from regarding their emancipation in any other light than that of a fight for mastery of the sources of production in which they must win by " downing " their present masters: in short, of class war. Thus the evil fate which we have seen dogging capitalism in foreign affairs pursues it pitilessly in home affairs also; and compels it to imbue its slaves with the very instinct of plotting, outwitting, over-reaching, grasping and fighting that makes revolution as inevitable as war. All the more reason for a vigorous disowning and discrediting of the profit-seeking motive, before its prevalence makes reasonable and peaceful social solutions impossible.

UNIVERSAL SABOTAGE

For consider what commercialization means. The capitalist, without the slightest hesitation, will destroy masses of useful products, or close down his works and abandon his employees to starvation in order to keep up prices. That is flat sabotage; and sabotage is a force that now threatens the existence of civilization. It is idle for the capitalist press to reserve the odious term for the parallel retaliations of the working class. In the running fight between Capital grasping at more profit, and Labor grasping at higher wages or desperately staving off a reduction, no moral distinction can be shown between the colliery owner who locks out his workmen from their livelihood and the workman who takes care that the locked-out mine shall be flooded for want of labor to pump it dry. The conspiracies by which the Trusts undersell and ruin small competitors until they have swallowed up a whole trade, and have the public at their mercy as to prices, are object-lessons to the combinations by which workmen make life impossible for the blackleg who takes less than the Trade Union rate of wage, or who sets a rate of working which gives the employer more than the market value for it. The authors of the silly jokes in our comic papers about bricklayers who lay two bricks a day forget that it is just as good business on capitalist principles for a bricklayer to reduce his tale of bricks as for his employer to cut wages. The limits to waste, to ca' canny, to sabotage, in short, to doing one's worst, are not moral limits in capitalism: they are economic limits set by the fact that if the ultimate consumer does not receive some value for his money he will not buy, and both employer and workman will be left destitute. But the demoralization of the parties is none the less complete because circumstances prevent them from reducing their immorality to absurdity. The habit of sabotage which it creates is growing on both of them with alarming rapidity.

Sensational instances will be found in the war of 1914-18, when successful invasion was accompanied as a matter of course by senseless sabotage; but there was nothing new in this. The peculiar form of sabotage which consists in simply burning the houses of economic opponents was practiced in the peasant wars of the fourteenth and sixteenth centuries, and revived with most dangerously suggestive success in the French Revolution and the establishment of the Irish Free State. The Luddite riots were so called, we are told, " after Ned Lud, a Leicestershire imbecile, who in a fit of passion demolished two stocking-frames." But the working men of 1811, the German general staff of

1914, and the Irish leader Michael Collins in 1920, did not regard Ned Lud as an imbecile, but as a strategist worthy of all imitation. We must face the practical certainty that if the transition from capitalism to socialism is not intelligently anticipated, planned and guided by the rulers of the people, the people, when the breaking strain is reached, will resort to sabotage to force whatever government may be left to tackle the job of reconstruction; and the danger is that the sabotage may go so far as to make the job impossible.

Consider, too, the unanswerable arguments placed by the war in the mouths of the saboteurs. They are told that trade is bad; that public enterprise is inefficient, corrupt, impossible and does not pay; and that they must tighten their belts and starve as best they may until trade revives. Their reply is crushing. They point out that when the government was confronted with the alternative of feeding and clothing them better than most of them had ever been fed and clothed in their lives before for four years, besides equipping them at enormous expense with instruments of destruction and slaughter, all out of the resources of the country, and yet retaining financial credit enough to borrow huge sums to lend to its allies, or else of having its throats cut by German bayonets, it discovered at once that all this was easily and lavishly possible. And they naturally, and quite soundly, conclude that the government could, *a fortiori,* feed and clothe and house and equip them for peaceful and fruitful production if the same steely incentive were applied. To this the constitutional parliamentary Labor leader has absolutely no reply except that as the saboteurs are incapable of organizing the throat-cutting as the German general staff organized it, the attempt would necessarily fail. Which again only throws the saboteur back on sporadic unorganized sabotage, wrecking of machines, blowing up of trains, burning of chateaux. Moral remonstrance and virtuous indignation are useless; if the game is to be one of pull-devil-pull-baker, and trading without conscience is to be the order of the day, capitalism need not hope to die quietly in its bed; it will die by violence, and civilization will perish with it, from exhaustion.

It may be said that the capitalist system has survived worse times. But it did so because, as Mr. Maynard Keynes has said in ringing phrases, it bluffed the people morally. "I seek only to point out," said the Cambridge economist, "that the principle of accumulation based on inequality was a vital part of the pre-war order of society and of progress as we then understood it, and to emphasize that this principle depended on unstable psychological conditions which it may be impossible to re-create. It was not natural for a population, of whom so few enjoyed the comforts of life, to accumulate so hugely. The war has disclosed the possibility of consumption to all and the vanity of abstinence to many.

Thus the bluff is discovered; the laboring classes may be no longer willing to forgo so largely, and the capitalist classes, no longer confident of the future, may seek to enjoy more fully their liberties of consumption so long as they last, and thus precipitate the hours of their confiscation."[1]

It is time to realize that the great significance of Karl Marx, of whom so much ignorant nonsense is still current, is not that he revolutionized economics and political science, but that he called the moral bluff of capitalism. The theoretic mistakes of Marx are as patent nowadays as the mistakes of Moses; but nobody who has ever read the historical chapters of *Das Kapital* can ever again fall under the illusion that capitalists, as such, are morally respectable. Marx, in spite of all his pretentious blunders in abstract economic theory— blunders which were not even favorable to socialism— succeeded magnificently in suddenly turning the banners of capitalism with their seamy sides to the audience, and presenting the drama of modern civilization with the bourgeois as the villain of the piece. In our intercourse with the Soviet Government of Russia nothing puzzles and scandalizes our diplomatists more than the assumption of the Communists that the advantage of moral prestige is on their side, and the impossibility of impressing any sort of respect on the attitude

[1] *The Economic Consequences of the Peace,* by J. M. Keynes, 1920, p. 19.

of ironic tolerance which is their nearest approach to international courtesy. To the British Foreign Office this seems mere impudence. No more dangerously misleading mistake could be made. The capitalist (bourgeois, as he is now generically described on the continent) does actually stand convicted of moral inferiority before the working classes; and neither the constitutional socialist nor the gunman-saboteur has any respect for him, or any belief in his necessity as a pillar of society.

Thus the class war has come to be regarded as a holy war, not without strong grounds, as this book has shown. To assume, as our capitalist statesmen and their journalists commonly do, that the proletarian combatants must know themselves to be criminals, and are mere looters of society without any conscientious sanction, can only lead to a most perilous undervaluation of the strength and persistence of the revolutionary forces at work in the world. It leads directly to the careless and uppish conclusion that the remedy is simply an increase in the police force and in the stringency of the criminal law. Such measures can inflame and exasperate a popular moral force: they cannot control it. If the people are not convinced that the police are morally right, they will finally burn down the police station, and nobody will give evidence against them.

The Armageddon of Economic Creeds

The last thing we would desire is to play the alarmists; for if anger is a bad counsellor, panic is a worse. But we cannot shut our eyes to the fact that worse things than any sensible citizen thought possible ten years ago have happened and are still happening daily, because our obsolescent institutions have been allowed to strain human endurance to breaking point instead of being modified to suit contemporary demands and conditions. The state of things in many other countries is much worse than—as yet—in Great Britain. Large stretches of Central Europe are reverting to the pre-capitalist stage of a sparsely populated agricultural country, dotted with industrial centers in rapid disintegration, destitute, diseased and disorderly, and with a violent antagonism growing up between their industrial proletariats and the peasants who are now not masters of the situation, which is unfortunately unmastered (that is the whole trouble), but of the food supply and consequently of the subsistence of the town proletariats. This seems to be the case in Russia and in Austria; and it may become the case in a much more threatening way in Germany. Now we have seen that even when capitalism is at the height of its productivity, the slum centers of its activity are foci of disease, of disablement for agricultural life, and of unemployable destitute persons. If even their productivity is wrecked, the result is the state of things that existed in Germany after the Thirty Years War, when bands of famishing persons were plundering enraged peasants and being massacred by them. These horrors are not extinct: rather have we elaborated them by the pogrom, which, being an economic phenomenon, srtikes the Christian Armenian as mercilessly as the Jew.

To stave off this extremity of social disaster the Italian bourgeoisie are arming themselves to subjugate the proletariat by open violence. For some years past the capitalists of the United States have been waging quite extensive wars against the laborers' unions. In the latest dictionaries such words as Fascisti and Pinkertons have to be defined as the mercenary soldiers of capitalism. And this is at a moment when the capitalist recruiting sergeants find the world full of young men who have learnt no trade but the trade of the trenches, who are experts with the bomb and the rifle, and who have been broken in to hold human life cheap and the value of property negligible.

As against these private troops of private capitalism the proletarians and the revolutionary intellectuals are advising and carrying out wholesale sabotage of the capitalist system, precisely as the republicans in Ireland, when they were united against English rule, sabotaged their country gentlemen and the industrial proprietors into forcing the government to make Ireland a Free State, and as the republicans who dissent to that settlement are now continuing the sabotage in an effort to force a complete detachment of Ireland from the British Commonwealth of Nations. The sabotage may fail in the one case as it has succeeded in the other; but either way it is so destructive that it must recoil ruinously on all the parties. The instance is menacingly close to our own doors. The example of Ireland is much talked of on the Clyde, the Tyne, the Tees, the Taff and other centers of unemployment. And if men who build ships and hew coal are ripe for sabotage, men who build houses and factories, and make machinery, are not likely to be more scrupulous in making jobs for themselves by destroying their own work.

We must not console ourselves by saying, as both the Marxist and capitalist doctrinaires do, that all wars are economic wars, and that economic wars soon blow over. That is so far true that very few men—not enough to count against the police—will fight for an economic advantage when they are given enough to live on as well as they have ever been accustomed to live. But as we have already shown, Communism is a religion, and belief in property a creed. The conflict between them is inspired by moral abhorrence as well as by cupidity; and the press on both sides appeals to this moral abhorrence, and says as little as possible about the selfish motive. Just as it would have been very difficult to induce the English people and the German folk to slaughter one another for those economic considerations which were the real grounds of the war, and each had therefore to be persuaded that the other was not human but fiendish, so there would be little reason to fear a class war of any formidable extent if the combatants could not be persuaded that they were engaged in a righteous crusade against the enemies of mankind. This persuasion is already in full swing in the columns of the capitalist press: we are all conscious of it. What our governing classes are not conscious of is that exactly the same persuasion, backed by terrible evidence, is at work on the other side; and that the class war, if and when battle is joined in earnest, will be one of the wars of religion, and may be waged on a scale, and with a ferocity, a self-sacrifice, and a persistence which will make the religious wars of the seventeenth century seem mere riots by comparison. They may begin by attempts at an international boycott of persons professing particular economic views. The United States already excludes Bolshevists who are truthful or simple enough to announce themselves as such. Russia excludes professed Hundred-per-cent Americans. This is boycotting, the most oppressive form of sabotage. If it spreads from country to country it may prove the beginning of a conflict in which nationalism, freedom of travel and settlement, liberty of opinion, racial equality, and many other war cries, may serve as pretexts for drawing of the sword for the Armageddon between the dogmas of Communism and

Property—dogmas as irrelevant to any sane reconstruction of the industrial order as were Free Will and
Necessity to the growth of the religious spirit.

The Moral Issue

We are thus brought to the conclusion that the failure of the reign of capitalism, as the principal form of
the nation's industrial and social organization, must
now be recognized and admitted. It is not merely this
or that excess or defect that stands condemned by the
world's experience. The making of pecuniary profit
has proved to be a socially injurious and even a dangerous stimulus to activity. The very motive of pecuniary gain, on which Adam Smith taught the whole
world to rely, is not one by which human action can be
safely inspired. After a whole century of trial, the
dictatorship of the capitalist for the purpose of private
gain has failed to commend itself to the judgment of
democracy throughout the world. And to-day the
Christian Church is driven to proclaim its agreement
with democracy. Addressing the English Church Congress in 1922, the Archbishop of York thus delivered
the Christian judgment on the " vast system of beliefs
and practices and policies, industrial, political, international, . . . which we may roughly call Western
civilization. It reached its zenith in the last century.
It was admirably contrived for the production of wealth

and power. With magnificent enterprise it yoked to its service the discoveries of science. It created and satisfied a thousand new demands of comfort and convenience. It called into being a vast industrial population. It stimulated patriotism by its belief in the survival of the strongest. But its motives, governing individuals and classes and states, were non-Christian self-interest, competition, the struggle of rival forces. Now these motives have over-reached themselves. They are breaking the fabric which they built. Surely the truth of this is writ large in the outbreak of the Great War and the perils of Europe to-day. The fabric itself cannot be overthrown without disaster. But if it is to be a blessing, not a blight, to mankind, its motives must be transformed." [1]

We suggest that—as with the last great aggression of the Hohenzollerns and their military advisers—it would have been a lasting calamity had the result been otherwise. The failure of capitalism is a good thing for humanity. The victory of irresponsible power over the lives of the mass of the people, even if it were confined to "economic" power, would have been a moral catastrophe. Whatever may be thought as to the indispensability of the motive of profit-making, no one ventures to assert that it is a high motive, or a noble aspiration. It admittedly does not lead to the produc-

---

[1] "Congress Sermon" at the English Church Congress, *Times*, October 11, 1922.

tion of art and beauty; it is a mockery of justice; it is inimical to friendship; it is not the parent of love. Even the keenest profit-maker instinctively resists the introduction of this all-powerful motive into his own family relations, in which a diametrically opposite set of principles is allowed to prevail. This "truce of God" is popularly extended to pecuniary relations between connections, between personal friends, and even to some slight extent between members of the same occupation or social class. Whole professions, indeed, make a pride of repudiating the profit-maker's creed as regards their own services. The army, the navy, the doctors, the clergy, the teachers, the judges, the fire brigade, police, and, in fact, all the salaried officers of the community have at no time accepted the making of profit as the guide to conduct in their own vocations. Moreover, by a peculiar illogic, the motive of securing personal profit has, in Britain at any rate, never been supposed to govern those who directed the affairs of state; and the cabinet minister, the colonial governor, the ambassador, the member of Parliament, the town councilor, or the justice of the peace who has aimed at the making of profit for himself out of the public service, has always earned, like Simon Magus, not public approval but public contempt. No doubt the opposite taste can be acquired. We recall the remark of a commercially-minded youth who was temporarily acting as secretary to one of these devoted and entirely unpaid

county administrators on whom so much of our social
organization depends. He disliked, he said, "this
morbid atmosphere of public work, with its everlasting
thinking of other people's needs." He longed to get
back to the more satisfying occupation of totaling up
the weekly profits of his father's shop. The socialist,
whilst by no means despising full maintenance for himself and his family (and, in fact, demanding it for every
one), feels a profound dislike for greed of gain as the
dominant motive; he demands that the "desire for
riches" shall no longer be made the basis of our statecraft, no longer preached to the young as the guide to
conduct, no longer applauded and honored as conducive
to the commonwealth. He believes that in the countries
advanced in civilization mankind is ready for a change
of heart, for the substitution of the motive of fellowship and public service for that of pecuniary self-
interest and the craving for riches. He does not
thereby demand any fundamental change in human
nature. What the establishment of a genuine coöperative commonwealth requires in the way of an advance
in morality is no more than that those who have the
gift for industrial organization should be, not saints
nor ascetics, but as public-spirited in their work, and
as modest in their claims to a livelihood, as our quite
normally human scientific workers, teachers in schools
and colleges, our whole army of civil servants of every
degree and kind, municipal officers of every grade, the

administrators of the consumers' coöperative movement, and the officials of the trade union world. And this substitution of the motive of public service for the motive of self-enrichment will be imposed on our consciences by the moral revolution, which will make " living by owning " as shameful as the pauperism of the wastrel; and will, moreover, regard the exceptionally gifted man who insists on extorting from the community the full " rent of his ability " as a mean fellow— as mean as the surgeon who refuses to operate except for the highest fee that he can extract. Even among the socially unscrupulous, the perception that the idle or useless life is neither healthy nor happy; that the amusements substituted for work are mostly devices for pillage by tradesmen; and that the troubles brought by property would be unendurable if the alternative were not poverty and degradation, seems to be growing. However that may be, there is abundant evidence that the necessary tasks of the world will get done, that inventions will be made, improvements introduced and duty performed, even if no man can hope, by persistently getting the better of his fellow-men, to accumulate a fortune. Owing to the advance of science and the growth of professional ethics it is now practicable—it is, indeed, essential if civilization is to be saved from disaster—to substitute for the Court of Profit the twin Courts of Efficiency Audit and Professional Honor.

But even if the evidence on this point were not yet complete, the socialist would still strive for the substitution of fellowship for fighting, of professional ethics for competitive trading, of scientifically audited vital statistics for the test of pecuniary profit, because to him the state of mind that is produced by fellowship and the pursuit of knowledge, the society in which fellowship is the dominant motive, and scientific method the recognized way, is—whether or not it is materially better provided—infinitely preferable to that produced by the economic war of man against man, and the social rancors, national and international, which are the outcome of such warfare.

Here we break off our diagnosis of the decay of capitalist civilization. Though we have been active members of the Labor and Socialist movement for over thirty years, we have never before framed an indictment of the capitalist system. Our time and energy have been devoted to municipal administration, to research into the facts of social organization, and to devising and advocating measures by which the existing profit-making system may be replaced, with the least political friction and the most considerate treatment of " established expectations," by a scientific reorganization of industry as a democratically controlled public service. We have pursued this course because we have no mind for denials that carry no affirmations, for demolitions that provide for no constructions. We have never felt free to preach an ideal until we have found the way towards its realization. But having done our best to survey the path to within sight of the goal, we may, without misgiving or malice, tell capitalism plainly what History will think of it when all the demagogues of our day are dead and forgotten. Those who will take the trouble to follow the rise and growth of the industrial and social institutions which, we believe, should and will gradually supersede the reign of capitalism can do so in our other writings, whether relating to the development of local government, to the organization and functions of trade unionism and the consumers' coöperative movement, to the increasing elaboration of factory legislation, and the enforcement of the policy of a National Minimum, or to the systematic prevention (as distinguished from the mere relief) of destitution.[1] And we think we may fairly claim that the careless accusation that socialists avoid details, and fail to work out in practicable projects the alternatives which they desire, does not apply to us, any more than it does to the publications of the British Labor Party and the Fabian Society.

But our former abstention from a moral judgment of capitalism can be justified only by belief that those who are in control of the government and the legislation of the country are aware of the gravity of the social diseases from which we are all suffering, and—what

[1] See the pages at the end of this volume.

is no less important—of the way in which these evils are regarded by the wage-earners, who constitute, in Britain, four-fifths of the population. Before the Great War there seemed to be a substantial measure of consent that the social order had to be gradually changed, in the direction of a greater equality in material income and personal freedom, and of a steadily increasing participation, in the control of the instruments of wealth-production, of the wage-earning producers and the whole body of consumers. This acquiescence in the progressive development of political and industrial democracy was manifested, during the generation that preceded 1914, not only in the extension of the suffrage to the wage-earning class, the abolition of the absolute veto of the House of Lords and the successive legislative affirmations of the right of free association, but also in the effective democratization of local government; in the steady extension of municipal services; in the systematization and nearly universal extension of factory and mines legislation; in the establishment, for millions of workers, of a legal minimum of wages as of a legal maximum of hours of labor, and last—and perhaps most important of all—in the progressive allocation of a steadily increasing share of the national income to the needs of the children, the sick and infirm, and the aged through old-age pensions and the public services of education, health and recreation. We thought, perhaps wrongly, that this characteristic British acquiescence on the part of a limited governing class in the rising claims of those who had found themselves excluded both from enjoyment and control, would continue and be extended willingly or reluctantly, still further from the political into the industrial sphere; and that whilst progress might be slow, there would at least be no reaction. But apparently the immense destruction of wealth by the war, and the helpless position into which the wage-earners throughout the world have been brought through the unemployment caused by the nature of the Peace, has both incited and encouraged the capitalists and landowners of Britain, as of the United States, some of them excited beyond all prudence by enormous war profits, to make a deliberate attempt to drive back the mass of the population, always on the most plausible commercial grounds, behind the positions gained during the last half century. Not only have wages been drastically reduced and hours of labor increased, *even in establishments continuing to make exceptional profits;* but the proportion of the national income allocated to such vital communal services as health and education has been diminished in order to reduce the income tax. In every industrial district the overcrowding of families in insanitary and often indecently occupied tenements is becoming more scandalous than even in the days of Lord Shaftesbury. The definite promises of Cabinet Ministers in 1918-19 to nationalize the railways and mines have been shamelessly broken. Instead of extending, according to the policy of the National Minimum, the operations of the highly successful Wages Boards, these bulwarks of the basic wage are being silently attenuated, or their powers undermined. There is in preparation an even more invidious attack on popular liberties; we are threatened, on the one hand, with the reëstablishment of the veto of an effective Second Chamber, expressly in order to resist further " concessions to labor "; and, on the other, with the practical withdrawal from the trade unions of their statutory right to determine by majorities their industrial and political activities. Up and down the country, in factory, shipyard and mine, it is being said and believed that these two measures are intended to " torpedo " both political and industrial democracy—thus driving the wage-earners to resort to " direct action " on an unprecedented scale. Such a counter-revolution, in the long run even more dangerous to those who are engineering it than inhibitive to the oceanic moral tide it vainly dreams of turning back, is made possible, we believe, partly by the ignorance of the British capitalist entrepreneur as to the strength of the case that can be made out against the continuance of his dictatorship, and partly by the blindness of the resentment which drives the proletarian to seek his remedy in the ruin of his economic antagonist and the destruction of the machinery which has enslaved him, rather than in the recognition that there is a better way for both. In an attempt, possibly vain, to make the parties understand their problem and each other better—in the hope that it is not always inevitable that Nature should harden the hearts of those whom she intends to destroy—we offer this little book.

INDEX

Adams, C. F., 22
Adams, John, 22
Adams, Messrs., 133
Adulteration as a form of competition, 124-130
Advertisement Consultants, Incorporated Society of, 141
Africa, 136, 204-206
Agriculture, Board of, 127
"Allowance System," the, 178
America, capitalism in, 3, 6, 17, 84-85, 145, 154; Civil War in, 177; manners in, 45-47
——, North, advertising in, 141; in eighteenth century, 165; slave trade in, 114
——, Southern, slave trade in, 9
——, Western, British markets in, 103
Amery, L. S., M.P., 209
Angell, Norman, 67
Anglican Church, 94
Antipodes, British markets at the, 103
Appomattox Court House, 9
Armageddon of economic creeds, 222-232
Arnold, Dr., 200
Arnold, Matthew, 46
Atholl, Duchess of, 11
Australia, capitalism in, 183; government employees in, 163; social conditions in, 12, 13, 43, 87; Labor and Socialist parties in, 214
Austria, 140
Authority, principle of, 60-63; problem of, 189-191

Babunin, 97
Bannington, B. G., 128
Bedlam, 22

Beer, M., 11
Belgium, Labor and Socialist Party in, 214
Belloc, Hilaire, 67
Bevan, Phillips, 128
Birmingham, County Court proceedings at, 133
Bismarck, Prince, 112, 206-208
Bluff, the capitalist, 74-77
Bolshevists, 119, 213, 225
Booth, Charles, 88, 185, 212
Bowley, A. L., 15
Brain-workers, position of the, 68-71; as salaried servants, 158-164
Brand, —, M.P., 167
Brennus, the sword of, 68
Bright, John, 10
British Commonwealth of Nations, 223
British Constitution, the, 59
British Economic Imperialism, 204-208
British Empire, the, 196, 209
British Medical Association, 132
British socialism, 112

Calgary, 122
Camden Society, 179-180
Canada, 122, 140
Capitalism, adverse developments of, 108-193; initial success of, 78, 181-187; destruction of the means of production by, 112-116; ruin of resources by, 119; case against, 181-187
Capitalist system, definition of, x, xi
Carlyle, Robert, 18
Carnegie, Andrew, 215

237

Carolinas, the, 42, 121
Cecil, Lord Hugh, 158
Chamberlain, Rt. Hon. Joseph,
M.P., 196-197, 209
Charity Organization Society,
171
Chartered South African Com-
pany, 207
Chartist Movement, 169, 175,
211
China, British markets in, 103;
opium trade with, 186, 200-
201
Christian Church, doctrines of,
10, 46, 206-207
Christian medieval civilization,
ix
Civilizations, the passing away
of, ix
Clarke, William, papers of,
179-180
Class war, the, 211-227
Clyde, the, 224
Coalition Government of 1920-
23, 209
Cobden, Richard, 7, 10, 204
Collins, Michael, 218
Colonies, trade combination in
the, 154
Colquhoun, Patrick, 11
Combination Laws, the, 97
Common Law, the, 99
Communism, 115, 219, 223, 224
Company Acts, 92
Conquistador, the, 206
Conservative Party, the, 158,
171, 189
Consumption, inefficiency of,
22; as seen by the Cosmical
Inspector, 23-25
Coöperative Wholesale Socie-
ties, 136
Costs increased by capitalism,
147-148
Court of Profit, 157, 184, 188-
189
"Court of Public Audit," the,
157
Crimean war, 10

Cromer, Lord, 199
Cromwell, Oliver, 179-180
Cuban war, the, 207

Dalton, Hugh, 15
Darcy, Jean, 207
da Vinci, Leonardo, 44
Daylight saving as scientific
consumption, 30
Demand, vitiation of effective,
28-30
Denmark, Labor and Socialist
Party in, 214
Dibblee, G. B., 67, 132, 140, 146
Dictatorship of the capitalist,
54-77; in government, 67-
68
Distributive State, the, 164
Divine Right of Kings, princi-
ple of, 207
Dresden, 211
Dysgenic effect of inequality,
49-52

East, trading in the, 143
Eastern civilization, 83
Egypt, ix, 76, 204
Electrical trades, Board of
Trade Reports on, 153
Elizabethan Poor Law, 166-
168. See Poor Law
Ely, Professor R. T., 123, 156
Engineering trades, Board of
Trade Report on, 153-154
Environment, dictation of the,
63-66
Equality before the law, 55-57
Europe, capitalism in, 9, 111,
141, 144, 158-161, 209; credit
system of, 198-199; news-
paper press in, 67
——, Central, disintegration of,
220-221
European civilization, xii, 3, 6

Fabian Society, publications of,
15
Factory Acts, 115
Fascisti, the, 223